The Dance Teacher's Survival Guide

?

The Dance Teacher's Survival Guide

Teaching Dance in schools
from Key Stage 1 – Key Stage 3

Kathryn Sexton
Illustrations by Mark Palmer

Dance Books
Alton

First published in 2004 by Dance Books Ltd,
The Old Bakery, 4 Lenten Street, Alton, Hampshire GU34 1HG
www.dancebooks.co.uk

Production by Liz Morrell & Patrick Donnelly
Printed by Latimer Trend & Company Ltd

ISBN: 1 85273 102 8

To my parents Len and Pat

This book has come about as a result of work that I have done with many non-specialist dance teachers in the London Borough of Bromley. I thank all colleagues, past and present, who have discussed, tried out and given feedback on ideas presented in this book.
My thanks also to my husband, John, and parents, Len and Pat, for their constant support.
I am indebted to Rosemary Pharo for her work on the presentation of this resource. I thank her sincerely for her belief in me and for all her time, advice, encouragement and wonderful IT skills. My thanks also to Mark Palmer for his great illustrations. Finally, my thanks to Dance Books Ltd for their work in the production of this book.

The Dance Teacher's Survival Guide is also dedicated to all those teachers who are faced with teaching their students dance as part of the national curriculum, but who have no specialist dance training.

This book shows you how to do it.

Contents

Introduction

What is it about teaching dance that makes some teachers want to run a mile?

I suppose the main issue is that it is perceived as a very personal thing. Perhaps it brings back childhood memories of Saturday morning dance classes and self-consciousness. Sometimes perhaps it's just the fact you don't have a structure for teaching it and you feel you haven't learnt the vocabulary. Maybe you love dance and movement, but don't have enough technical information. Or maybe you simply think that to teach dance requires higher levels of creativity than you believe you possess.

Well, the fact is, that given the information, tools and techniques in this book, you will be able to teach dance confidently from Key Stage 1 to Key Stage 3. And once you have found your confidence, all the Key Stage 3 units could also work easily at Key Stage 4.

This method shows you how to:

- Structure a dance lesson at each Key stage
- Do effective warm ups at each Key Stage
- Time each part of the lesson
- Develop a basic vocabulary for dance movements
- Prepare lesson outlines from models you can copy and use
- Use music

I generally recommend that you develop and feel comfortable with one basic approach to teaching dance such as the one I have presented in detail. This is known as motif and development and is the most common method dancers use to make dances. Once you are more confident, you naturally develop your own methods. The main thing to remember is that:

- The children are usually more creative than you are
- Your job is to provide the stimulus for their creativity and to keep a structure to activity in the lesson
- There are no rights and wrongs in creative dance
- DON'T PANIC

Using this book in lessons

You'll find the book divided into helpful sections: The first section gives you a basic toolkit for approaching dance lessons, the second section gives you lesson plans from Key Stages 1 – 4, including aims and outcomes. and the third section contains useful reference material.

The Dance Teacher's Toolkit

How to structure a dance lesson

Use the table below as a basic guide to the structure and timing of your dance lesson. The page numbers at the end of each line guide you to more detailed explanations and instructions for each section. It's as simple as that.

		Key Stage 1	Key Stage 2	Key Stage 3	See page
	Total lesson time	25 minutes	25 minutes	60 minutes	
1.	**Warm up time**	5 minutes	5 minutes	10 minutes	14
2.	**Creating/Composing**				
	Improvisation	5 minutes	5 minutes	10 – 25 minutes	22
	Selection and Development	8 minutes	8 minutes	15 –20 minutes	26
3.	**Performing**	3 minutes	3 minutes	5 minutes	36
4.	**Appreciating**	3 minutes	3 minutes	8 minutes	36
5.	**Cool down/Conclusion**	2 minutes	2 minutes	5 minutes	40

Talking the talk

Here's a basic outline of dance talk and what it means. At the end of the book is a fuller glossary of terms, but if you learn these basic ones now, you can understand and deliver all the lesson outlines included later in the book.

Asymmetric – the two sides of this shape are *not* a mirror image
Canon – performing the same movement one after each other – just as in a round in singing
Circle – tracing the shape of a circle with a body part
Contract – a squeezing action in the abdomen (as if punched in stomach)
Direction – up, down, sideways, forwards, back and diagonal
Drop – a sudden/heavy falling down of whole or part of the body
Duet – a dance for two people
Ease – move gently
Level – the height at which the movement is happening – i.e. head height, waist height, feet height etc
Lunge – a large step onto a bent leg leaving the back leg behind
Jump – an explosive movement from the feet taking the whole body into the air
Phrase – generally three to six movements joined together (see page xx)
Push up – pushing the body away from the floor with your hands
Roll – turning on the horizontal plane (like roly polys or rolling down a hill)
Sequence – a development of the phrase (see above) generally 6 – 12 movements joined together and approximately 20 – 30 seconds long (see page 26)
Spin – turning like a spinning top but keeping one body part in contact with the floor
Stretch – an extension of the whole or part of the body
Symmetric – two sides of a shape that are a mirror image
Structure – how a dance is organised
Swing – a movement with momentum – like the heavy swing of a pendulum
Turn – rotating the whole or part of the body on the vertical place
Unison – two or more dancers performing the same movement at the same time (as in singing in unison)
Walk – Stepping as in everyday life

Phrasing it right...

Dancers tend to talk a lot about 'phrases' and 'developing phrases'. The easiest way to explain what is meant is to compare it with a sentence. Where a sentence has words a dance 'phrase' has movements such as 'jump' or 'turn' – and that is all there is to it. Some phrases are complicated and some are very simple and that's all there is to it.

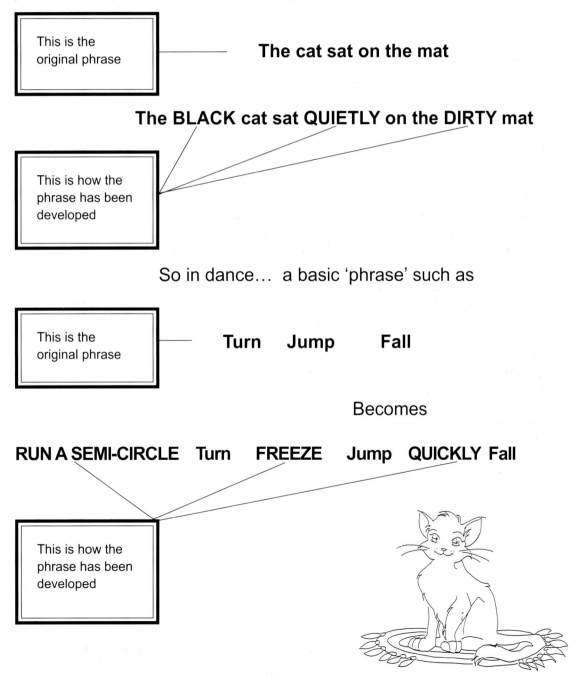

This is the original phrase

The cat sat on the mat

This is how the phrase has been developed

The BLACK cat sat QUIETLY on the DIRTY mat

So in dance... a basic 'phrase' such as

This is the original phrase

Turn   Jump   Fall

Becomes

RUN A SEMI-CIRCLE   Turn   FREEZE   Jump   QUICKLY Fall

This is how the phrase has been developed

Music

Do you find yourself spending far too much time trying to find 'just the right' piece of music? Well don't. Remember that your choice of music does not have to originate from the same idea as your dance idea – if you are making a dance based on, for example, war, you do not actually have to use music that has originated from or is based on war.

What you do want to do is use as wide a range of music/accompaniment as possible. Many children only listen to pop music and see dance only as the kind we see on pop videos. Or they assume dance just means ballet and has to be performed to classical music which they perceive as old fashioned. Dance lessons provide an opportunity to allow children hear (and hopefully enjoy) many different types of music opening their ears and eyes to many different musical soundworlds and broadening their whole experience of other cultures.

Most libraries have a reasonable selection of music from around the world. An interesting project would be to study the music and dance of one country, for example, India. Equally, you could take a piece of Indian music out of its geographic context and use it to accompany your work on an emotion – see *Improvisations using emotion*, p 25. Film and television themes are also a useful source. The CD produced to accompany this book (see p.136) gives you some ideas and resources to use.

And remember that dance can also be performed very effectively to the spoken word e.g. poems, weather reports; natural sounds – rain, bird song; sound effects – creaking doors, footsteps; and natural noise – stamping, shouting. Another approach is to compose a piece of music with the children alongside their dance composition.

You do not need a specific piece of music or other accompaniment in mind at the onset at the project. You will find that ideas evolve alongside the composition. Experiment with different accompaniments, and then make your final decision. Don't be afraid to experiment and then ask the children. They will often surprise you.

Four steps to dancing

When dancers talk about dance they usually refer to four basic components of movement. These are:

- action
- space
- time
- dynamics

All the possibilities you will need for experimenting with, and developing movement ideas fall under these four headings.

ACTION (WHAT YOU DO)

Our bodies are able to move anatomically in three ways – flexion, extension and rotation. We combine these basic actions in many different ways to produce numerous movements. These are then commonly categorised under the following six headings:
- travelling – you run, walk or crawl, slide
- elevation – you jump, hop or leap
- turning – you turn, spin or roll
- gesture – you wave, reach or point
- stillness – you hold a position still (like a frozen waterfall)
- falling – you drop or fall

SPACE (WHERE YOU DO IT)

Dancers split these up into
- Level
- Direction
- Planes

Level

The three basic levels are low (near to the floor), medium (standing height) and high (above standing height). It is good practice to encourage children, from the word go, to create interest in their movement **by using a variety of levels**. Children new to dance will usually do everything at standing height. Using different heights in warm-up activities is a good way to get the ball rolling with this one. Where children are working in groups of two or more it can be very effective to have different members of the group performing shapes or actions at different levels.

Direction

Performing the same movement(s) to a new direction can give it a totally new look or even meaning. Some options are – forwards, backwards, sideways, circular, up, down and to the corners (diagonal). Where children are working in a group of two or more it can be very effective to have different members of the group doing the same movement but in different directions.

Planes

Movements can be performed in the following ways – up to down, side to side and forwards to backwards. When two of these dimensions are combined we call them planes of movement. There are three planes:

- Table plane (side to side + forwards to backwards) e.g. opening and closing
- Door plane (up to down + side to side) e.g. rising and falling
- Wheel plane (up to down + forwards to backwards) e.g. advancing and retreating

TIME (WHEN YOU DO IT)

The two elements here are:

- speed – how quickly you do the movement – fast or slow
- duration – how long you continue to perform the movement – sudden or sustained

DYNAMICS (HOW YOU DO IT)

I always think this is the hardest thing to explain to a class – I tend to say it is the energy or quality of the movement. It is a combination of weight + time + space.

Rudolf Laban, the dance pedagogue, devised a table of specific movement qualities which he called *effort actions*. This may seem a little technical, but it's actually quite straightforward. There are eight efforts and you'll find them listed on page 135.

Preparing the Space

The main two things to consider for your lesson are that the space is as clear as possible and that the temperature is comfortable.

Ideally there will not be any large obstacles in your teaching space that children could bang into (or jump off). If you do have items that are potentially hazardous such as a piano or trolley of mats, then the children need to be trained how to behave in the space. Use your first lesson to set very clearly the ground rules for expected behaviour. For this lesson it is **your** space and **you** are responsible for the children. Sanctions for inappropriate behaviour should be explained and applied. Get this right at the very start and life will be a lot easier in the long run.

Chairs should be stacked neatly and pushed to the very edge of the room so as not to be a distraction. If children change in the space before the lesson all bags and clothing should be removed and stored somewhere they cannot be accidentally trodden on. It is so easy to slip on a shirt, book or bag. If you have helpful site staff you may be able to make an arrangement with them to help prepare the space before your lesson. This is particularly important if you have a lesson straight after lunch in a space also used for eating. Nobody wants to roll on the floor and come face to face with an egg sandwich. You may even have a small team of responsible students who can help clear the space at the end of lunchtime.

Ideally the room will be warm enough so that children are not too cold in shorts and t-shirt. If a space is too cold there is an increased risk of injury as the muscles may not warm enough to stretch safely. If the children need to wear heavy jumpers or sweatshirts just to keep warm the clothing will interfere with the movement. (see *What to wear*). Similarly in the summer ensure there is adequate ventilation so the children do not overheat. If a space is too hot the children will be more lethargic and some may even feel lightheaded or dizzy. It certainly won't encourage them to work hard and get even hotter.

What to wear

The clothing worn for dance lessons should allow the children to move freely and easily. Their normal PE kit is usually fine.

- Try to avoid very heavy baggy clothing such as thick jumpers or track suit trousers that hide the line of the body

- Make sure any trousers do not hang below the ankle in case the children skid on them

- T-shirts and shorts or leggings are ideal

- Try to encourage all pupils to dance in bare feet. This will help strengthen their feet as they work harder than if they were in shoes, and also allows greater sensitivity and detail in their movement. Dancing in shoes is like trying to play the trumpet with gloves on. It also hurts a lot less if toes are accidentally trodden on.

Working with National Curriculum themes

Key Stage 1/Key Stage 2

Would you like to tie in your dance lessons to the theme you are working on in class? My suggestion is that you use Unit 3 (*Action Words*) as a basis and simply adapt the words to fit the subject. If you have resources such as stories, poems, films or pictures as part of your theme, then the unit to look at is Unit 1 (*Maori Legend*).

If you turn to Unit 3 on page 62, I have listed ideas for Pirates, Victorians, Egyptians and Electricity. You will also find ideas for using props and costumes there. Once you have got the hang of working this way, you'll find it easy to apply to virtually any theme you are using in the classroom.

Where to find more help

Dance companies often have educational outreach programmes which will come into schools and there are many other video and internet resources you can call upon in your dance teaching. We've listed a number of tried and tested sources in *Further Reading* and the *Resource Finder* (see pages 137 and 138).

Warming up

What is the warm-up section for?

There are two main purposes behind the warm up. Firstly, just as in any physical exercise, you are looking to raise the body temperature, loosen joints and pre-stretch muscles to avoid injury, and also to focus the mind and body for the demands of the lesson. Secondly what you may also be aiming to do is to re-cap ideas from previous lessons, find movement ideas for the lesson or teach new movements.

Do I have to lead it from the front?

No. If you do not feel confident with dance you do not have to put yourself at the front and demonstrate. You can:

Talk the class through a series of tasks (see warm ups 2 & 3)

You can ask the pupils to suggest movements that the rest of the class copy (see warm up 1)

You can pose questions that pupils answer by making movements (see warm up 1)

I am comfortable demonstrating movement

You can demonstrate movements that the class copies (see warm up 4)

You can demonstrate and teach a sequence of movements (see warm up 5)

Five basic approaches to warm ups

There are many different approaches to warm ups. Listed below are five different approaches that you can use as they are or use as a springboard.

Watch out for children suggesting movements that are too big and explosive for the start of a lesson. there may be a risk of injury and over-excitement in the class

Warm-up idea 1

What you do	What you say	Look out for/notes
Get the whole group to stand in a circle with you Get them to suggest warm-up ideas. They demonstrate, the rest of the class follows	Can anyone suggest a simple movement to loosen or stretch one part of our body? Let's see what part of our body we can circle Can you take that circling down low or up high? Can you move it away from the circle or come back to it?	You may wish to start this activity: have a few ideas e.g. circling heads, shoulders, elbows, wrists, knees ankles etc. As pupils suggest, you can add in extra ideas such as changing the level or direction

Especially useful if you are going to work on turning actions later in the lesson

Instead of circling you could substitute:

- body parts that swing
- two different body parts making contact
- body parts being stretched then bent
- body parts that shake

Warm-up idea 2

What you do	What you say	Look out for/notes
Send the pupils on a journey around the dance space	Stand still in your own space in the room. Look at another point in the room, walk purposefully towards it. Stop. Turn to look at another spot in a different direction. Move backwards at a low level to that point. Stop. Turn to look at another spot... continue changing the instruction for the journey each time with – • fastest and most direct route • gentle and wiggly route • do a turn and a jump on route • reverse the last route you did • do last route extra large in slow motion • freeze half way for four seconds	Pupils combine walking, jumping, turning and rolling. Make sure their journeys have a focus and a sense of purpose Pause before each change of direction to re-focus (longer for younger children, shorter for older) Keep the speed down to avoid clashes. Constantly remind class to move to spaces and be aware of where other people are

This is especially useful when you are working on different actions later in the lesson as it gets the children thinking of movements

Developing the idea

Ask the children to think of actions between the walking other than jumping, turning or rolling.

For instance they could:

* swing or stretch whole body or body parts
* find a way to use at least one hand to travel
* twist, balance and tip, 'melt' or 'explode' into travelling movements
* work in pairs to perform it as a kind of 'follow my leader' activity

Further development

* work individually or in pairs to make a journey
  (using the previous ideas) with four changes of direction
* the sequence must be repeatable
* perform each route of the journey in eight counts
* perform each route of the journey in four counts
* how about two counts?

Warm-up idea 3

What you do	What you say	Look out for/notes
Get the children to play games and activities they already know from e.g. the playground such as: Stuck in the mud. Start the game exactly as they are familiar with it. However when they get stuck the children have to make a particular shape such as *symmetrical/ asymmetrical* (see page 5) To 'release', you set a task such as sliding under/jumping over/ turning/copying the whole shape or one body part	We are going to play Stuck in the mud. James and Carol are going to be 'it'	Children are travelling, stopping, changing direction, holding still and strong shapes and changing level
	Everyone starts standing still in a space. When I say 'go' James and Carol will try to catch you. You can jog away from them to get avoid being caught. If they touch you on the shoulder you must stand still with your feet apart and arms to the sides in an asymmetric shape. Make the shape as strong as you can	Ensure the game doesn't get too fast or the class too over-excited. Use long pauses to change 'it' as a calming measure
	Others can release you by going under your legs	
	When I shout 'STOP' (blow whistle/bang drum) everybody must freeze. I will then choose two different people to be 'it.' Don't move until I say 'GO'	

This is especially useful when working on symmetry and asymmetry in a lesson or for re-inforcing a particular shape from a previous lesson e.g. curved, twisted, wide, narrow

Warm-up idea 4

Face the class and perform a series of warming/ stretching exercises. You should use a variety of exercises

What you do	What you say	Look out for/ notes
1) Use walking jogging, skipping ideas, arm rotation, swings and shaking different body parts	Shake your right/left arm. Harder. Take it above your head. Keep shaking. Now down below your knees. Shake your shoulders – up and down, now front and back. Shake your hips. Shake your right/ left leg. Wiggle your head. Now shake everything. Repeat sequence using circling or swinging actions.	You are aiming to raise body temperature and loosen muscles and joints gradually
2) Simple stretches - head and neck, arms/ trunk legs/ feet.	Turn your head to look right/left. Tip your right/left ear towards your right/left shoulder. Drop your chin down towards your chest. Stretch your arms above your head- try to keep your shoulders from lifting up too – imagine £10 notes hanging from ceiling. Reach up with right/left arms to grab the money. Stretch right up out of your waist. Open your arms as wide as you can. Give yourself a hug. Keep your feet in parallel (like train tracks). Take right/left leg back straight. Bend front leg and gently push heel of back foot towards floor. Lift right/left heel to bottom and push hip gently forwards.	Work from head to toe holding simple stretches for about five seconds each Move slowly into each stretch and hold. Be aware of pupils collapsing instead of extending in each stretch
3) Jumping	• Do three small jumps and one large jump touching your knees four times • Do eight springs from one foot to the other on the spot • Bend your knees and straighten (plie) • Bend your knees and jump to land having turned clockwise 90 degrees Repeat 3 more times turning 90 degrees in between each repeat to end facing front.	Ensure pupils bend knees to land and put heels down on each landing. Knees come up to chest not the other way round.

This is especially useful if you prefer to establish a set warm up routine for every lesson or you wish to teach a specific performance skill such as extension (i.e. stretching)

Warm-up idea 5

In this warm up, you teach a specific dance phrase that you are going to use as part of the movement later in the class. As part of the warm up you can teach the phrase:

- as a series of actions with no reference to the lesson theme. Actions from the phrase can be referred to later in the lesson when you introduce the theme.

OR

- as a way of introducing the theme with images being used from the start to get the quality of movement.

For example, your theme is:

The qualities of water

Key Stage 1	
1. Trace three soft slow circles with your right arm	Image of ripples in a pond
2. Slowly look to the right slightly nodding head, repeat to left, again to the right, again to the left	Image of trickling water
3. Drop suddenly into a crouch – make 'whoosh' sound with voice	Waterfall
4. Slowly stand reaching arms high about head	Water climbing to the crest of the fall
5. Repeat Step 3	Waterfall
6. Drop hips to floor and sit on bottom, legs out in front	
7. Rock from side to side on bottomusing your hands to take some weight	Waves

Key Stage 2

1. Make three circles with right shoulder, then elbow, then whole arm	Image of ripples in a pond
2. Slowly look to the right slightly nodding head, repeat left and circle head to end in curved shape	Image of trickling water
3. Drop suddenly and heavily to crouch position	Waterfall
4. Slowly stand reaching arms high about head, on tip toe repeat drop to different crouch position	Waterfall
5. Drop hips to floor and sit on bottom, legs out in front. Rock fromside to side four times using hands to take some weight	Waves
6. Roll 360 degrees (right across tummy and back to sitting)	Wave break
7. Take hands to floor on left side and drum fingers on floor	Rain
8. Slowly stand gently drumming fingers up body until still	Evaporation

Key Stage 3

1. Make a slow soft circle with your right arm over your head and then drop it down by your side	Image of ripples in a pond
2. Make a slow soft circle with your head leading into lunge with your left leg to left side, with a focus to left	Image of trickling water
3. Drop suddenly and heavily to floor in a crouch	Waterfall
4. Jump high, arms raised and land back in crouch position facing different direction	
5. Drop your hips to the floor – sit on bottom, then roll down until you are lying flat on your back	Image of water rippling
6. Rock from side to side on bottom using your hands to take some weight	Wave
7. Take hands to floor on left side and drum fingers on floor	Rain
8. Ease down and on to stomach in wide shape	Puddles
9. Push up from floor to finish sitting on heels	Evaporation
10. Slowly stand, head coming up last to face new direction	Evaporation
11. Start again	

Improvisation

If the burning question in your mind is 'How do I get the pupils to come up with ideas?' (and from experience, it often is), then here are four basic rules which should bring you good results. Together with the following section on selection, this part of the lesson is referred to as creating and composing.

The aim of improvisation is to explore different movement ideas. The teacher's role here is to guide their exploration and discovery and to encourage them not to always settle on the first idea they thought of. Ultimately the objective is to find a way to making a movement 'phrase' which can then be developed. It doesn't matter how basic the phrase is. Let the pupils work to their own levels. The younger/less able pupils will follow your step-by-step instructions. More able pupils will have the confidence to add their own ideas and soon begin to start choreographing small dance phrases in front of your eyes.

The golden rules for improvisation

- Make your task setting as structured and narrow as possible to begin with
  This will make the movement 'answer' clear to pupils
- Only set one task at a time
- Particularly with younger or less able children, your first task should be very specific – setting a wide-open task only causes confusion
- Only move on to the 'challenge' task with pupils who are ready to cope with it
  The signs to watch for are that the initial one or two closed tasks are answered well. This is a decision you might make yourself, or you could invite pupils to try the challenge if they would like to

As with warm ups, you can teach either from inside a circle or, if you are comfortable demonstrating, then from the front.

Improvisation at Key Stage 1
At this stage you are encouraging children to try out one or two possible movement answers and then choose their favourite. e.g. Individually: 'Show me a very wide shape' 'Now show me another wide shape that looks completely different' 'Choose the best one to show to the rest of the class'.

Improvisation at Key Stage 2
At this stage you are encouraging children to try three or four possible movement answers and choose perhaps two they feel work best e.g. In pairs: 'From the wide shapes we have tried individually, choose two that are different but look good close together.' 'Now both make a new wide shape with space between you.'

Improvisation at Key Stage 3
At this stage you are encouraging children to explore several fuller movement answers to the same task and make judgements about them. e.g. Individually: From the wide shapes we have tried pick one from each level – low, medium and high and move through a curled position to arrive at each shape. Try to choose wide shapes that contrast with each other to add interest.

1. Improvising using pathways
Getting from A to B
'Curved and straight pathways'

Suitable for: Key Stage 1 & Key Stage 2

Underlying idea: All movements in dance follow 'pathways'. This simple improvisation exercise gets pupils to actively think about how they can move different parts of their bodies from A to B. This is also a way to introduce the idea of pathways. (see *Glossary*) At Key Stage 3 you can call these 'floor and air patterns.' (see *Colour and Shape* unit page 99).

What you do: Begin by asking the pupils to find the longest and most fun way to get their hand from above their heads at A to sitting on it with their bottom at B.

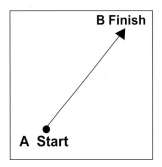

Task 1

What you say
Begin with your hand above your head at A and find the longest and most fun way to finish by sitting on it at B

Challenge tasks
*   Can your hand move over/under other parts of your body such as an arm or leg?
*   Does your hand make your head/back/legs move differently at all?
*   Does your hand always travel in the same direction or does it sometimes go backwards, up or down?
*   Does your hand always have to move at the same speed?

Once your pupils have practised and remembered this 'pathway', move on to Task 2

Task 2

What you say

I'd like you to find a way of moving from where you are now, A, to a totally new part of the room, B.

Challenge tasks

*   Will the travelling always be only on your feet?
*   Will it always be forward?
*   Will it always stay at the same speed?
*   Can a certain part of your body lead the way e.g. elbow, hips, shoulder

Variations of the tasks
Suitable for Key Stage 2 & Key Stage 3

*   These tasks could then be repeated using the most straight and direct pathway
*   Make A the right hand touching the left foot and B feet apart with right hand stretch sideways at shoulder level

Developing more challenge tasks

Once the pupils understand the difference between straight and curved pathways, you could say:

*   Choose where you want to start your journey and where you'd like to finish your journey. Then choose which part of your body is going to lead you there
*   The first time I'd like you to make a curved pathway
*   The second time I'd like you to make a straight pathway

Further developments
Most suitable for Key Stage 3

Get them to perform the whole journey in reverse from B to A.
Work in pairs and say:
*   'copy your partner's journey',
*   'mirror your partner's journey'
*   'make up three different pathways and then join them all together'

Notes

By joining three different parts together, the pupils have composed a whole dance phrase.

2. Improvising using emotions, e.g. anger

Suitable for: Key Stage 2 & Key Stage 3
Underlying idea: Movement can be a very effective way of expressing an emotion or feeling. Different kinds of movement can suggest different moods and the way we perform them can express how we are feeling. This exercise allows children to begin to explore the notion of movement communicating meaning.

What you do
Begin by talking about how it feels to be angry.
What makes you angry?
What do you do when you are angry? – stamp foot, point, lean forward, scowl.
Possibly show pictures of angry faces (newspapers are a good source).
Ask children to find simple movement and shapes that show some of those angry feelings.

Task 1

What you say
* 'I'd like you to sit on the floor and show me one quick movement that tells me that you are angry, for example, stamp your foot' (or substitute which ever emotion you choose to explore)
* 'Stand facing away from me and show me another'
* 'Hold one pose still to tell me you're angry with me'

Task 2

Repeat Task 1 with a partner showing you are angry with each other.

Challenge tasks

Stand away from, but facing, your partner, still showing anger
* move towards each other slowly into an anger pose
* drop to the floor and roll away quickly to finish just staring at each other with 'the evil eye'
* stand and jump towards each other and do an angry movement one after each other
* think of a way to move quickly away from each other and finish pointing at each other

Notes:
Children may well need help moving from one movement to the next. We call these transitions. Encourage them to keep transitions simple to start with – this usually means moving quite slowly. e.g. from A to B = end A standing, bend knees to crouch position and use hands on floor to help balance, then put bottom on floor and roll across bottom. The most important thing is that they are safe. As they become more confident they may experiment with more complex transitions, e.g. from A to B = end A standing, turn, jump and land in crouch position, then put bottom on floor and swing legs behind to end lying on tummy, roll 360 degrees to end on tummy again.

Selection and development

This is the creative heart of the lesson. All other sections work towards it and from it.

Selection

Having allowed the pupils to improvise or 'play' with movement ideas earlier in the lesson, your aim, as the teacher, is to guide them towards forming a short, basic movement phrase which can then be developed in the ways I describe in the next section.

Help the children make decisions about the look and quality of their work. Get them used to the idea of not settling for the first idea they think of. The first idea is often the easiest but not necessarily the most interesting or challenging. It is good practice for the children to be involved in decision-making about their work from the start.

The image I use when I teach is a choreography 'bucket'. At the start of a unit or lesson the 'bucket ' is empty. Our first job is to put some movement ideas into the bucket. (This is done by following the ideas from the **Warm up** and **Improvisations** sections so far). Once we have a few different ideas in the bucket we can pick out the ones we would like to keep and join them together to make our basic phrase, for example, working on wide and narrow shapes.

Selection at Key Stage 1

At Key Stage 1 they only need two ideas in the 'bucket' at a time and then choose one to keep. You may repeat this two or three times to make the phrase.

e.g. Through improvisation tasks children will have made two or three wide shapes. They have to choose their favourite. Then improvise with narrow shapes in the same way and ask them to choose one. Ask them to perform the wide shape, then the narrow shape. Ask them to pick one more shape they have made to go on the end (wide or narrow). Their phrase will consist of three movements.

Selection at Key Stage 2

At Key Stage 2 they could have three or four ideas in the 'bucket' at a time and choose two to keep. You may repeat this to create a longer phrase.

e.g. Through improvisation children will have made three or four wide shapes. Ask them to pick two and perform them one after each other. Do the same for the narrow shapes. They now have four shapes. Ask them to decide an order for the shapes e.g. WIDE, NARROW, WIDE, NARROW. This is their basic phrase.

Selection at Key Stage 3

At Key Stage 3 they could have five or six ideas in the 'bucket' at a time and choose three or four to make the phrase.

e.g. Through improvisation children will have made five or six wide shapes. Ask them to choose two or three. Do the same for the narrow shapes. They now have between four to six shapes. Ask them to decide an order for the shapes. e.g. WIDE, NARROW, NARROW, WIDE, NARROW, WIDE.

How do they choose what to take from the bucket?

- you ask them to choose their favourite movement(s)
- you ask them to include a movement that you taught the whole class
- they show a partner their ideas and the partner suggests which one(s) to keep
- they choose two ideas that contrast with each other e.g. at different levels
- they choose their most original movement(s)
- they choose the movement(s) that they think best shows the stimulus idea e.g. anger
- you video their ideas and they watch themselves before choosing

Development

Now you have got the basic phrase of movement together, you can build on it. If we use the analogy of making a cake – if 'selection' is putting the cake together, then 'development' is icing and decorating it. Like icing and decorating, this part can be great fun for both pupils and teachers.

Your aim is to guide the children through the process of:

- making the movement phrase longer by adding/repeating movement
- changing the speed of some of the movement – fast, medium, slow
- changing the quality/effort of some of the movement to add interest, e.g. smooth and light or sudden and direct
- including a variety of level to add interest – low, medium, high
- facing different directions to add interest – front, back, side, diagonal
- playing/experimenting with repeating actions in different orders to add interest

Development at Key Stage 1

Keep all the class working on one development task at a time. Guide the pupils through three or four developments of their original phrase.

Development at Key Stage 2

Keep all the class working on one development idea at a time e.g. speed, but give them the opportunity to include more than one response. Guide them through four or five developments.

Development at Key Stage 3

Keep all the class working on one development idea to begin with but work towards being able to instruct them to develop more than one at a time e.g. Task = your phrase must include one change of direction, a change of level and at least one change in speed. Aim for consideration of variety in speed, level, direction to become second nature for them. Guide them through seven or eight developments.

Basic approaches to development

Remember the four basic components of movement (action, space, time, dynamics) from *Four steps to dancing* page 9. This is where they really come into their own.

Action
- Develop movement phrases by asking children to add in new actions – either before or after a particular movement. e.g. if the original movement was a turn they could

- jump in narrow shape, land and turn
- turn and crouch down making a low wide shape
- join together a jump, land, turn, crouch, shape
- Ask children to think of a new action to move into or out of a movement they already have

Space
- Ask the children to repeat/adapt a movement on a different level

Direction
- Ask the children to repeat a small phrase of movement to a new direction

Plane
- Ask the children to make an action or shape with a different body part. Asking children to adapt movement in this way is probably more suitable for Key Stage 3 as the concept of the planes is quite hard for younger children to understand

Floor and air patterns
- Ask the children to transfer an air pattern to a floor pattern or vice versa. Floor and air patterns are something all children can understand. We can use the whole or just part of our body to make or trace different kinds of patterns. Those patterns can be as if we were 'writing' on a wall (air pattern) or as if we were 'writing' on the floor (floor pattern). Those patterns could be straight or curved lines, circles, zigzags, alphabet letters, mathematical shapes, spirals or squiggles. A simple development could be to repeat an air pattern on the floor or vice versa. Leading with a different body part as well often results in a completely new movement idea. e.g. The original movement is tracing an air pattern of a zigzag with the right elbow. This becomes tracing the biggest zigzag possible as a floor pattern leading with the left heel. Perhaps ask them to join together the two ideas with a new action, such as a jump to face a new direction

Movement Size
- Changing the size of movement(s) is a common development idea. Children rarely think to change the scale of the movements they do and will opt for what feels most comfortable. It can be great fun to ask children to repeat a movement they have thought of, except do it ten times bigger or ten times smaller. The results will amaze you. In order to do it bigger they may well have to run, walk, jump or leap and it will take longer. In order to do it smaller they may need to do it with just a finger, their eyes or even their nose. Asking children to repeat a movement idea in a different size is an effective development task

Time
- Ask children to add or repeat movement at a different speed
  Repeating or finding new movement(s) with changes to either of these elements can again produce interesting results. Once again children will naturally think of movement with a very medium, comfortable pace. Making the movement much quicker or slower

will often alter the whole energy of the movement and make them perform it in a completely different way. Suddenly 'exploding' into a movement can be dramatic or 'yawning' into it can be soothing or perhaps suggest a struggle

Dynamics
- Ask children to alter the dynamics of a movement. This probably has the most radical effects. For ideas for specific movement qualities see *Laban's Effort Table* on page 137

Other development ideas
You ask the children to:
- Work in pairs and learn each other's movement. Join the two together so you can both perform the whole dance
- Watch another pair/group and pick out one or two movements to put in your dance
- Watch a short extract from a video and pick out two movements to add into your dance
- One pupil teaches a successful movement idea to the whole class and they add it into their dance

Developing the Waterfall Study (pages 19-21)

Here's an example of how to take the *Waterfall Study* and develop it. You can then apply the same kind of ideas to any other phrases the children develop.

Key Stage 1

WHAT YOU DO

Ask them to perform 'the waterfall' : drop to crouch position ('whoosh') & slowly stand reaching arms high

Guide them through four simple developments as a whole class

WHAT YOU SAY

a) Let's do our 'waterfall' together and try to keep exact time with each other

b) Now let's try to make this more exciting. Let's rise up on our toes before we drop down

c) Can you rise up very slowly? Try taking a big breath in. Bring your hands up to your shoulders as you do it

d) Now make that drop/'whoosh' as fast as you can. Let out all that big breath as you say 'whoosh'

e) Now let's see if we can turn in a circle as we stand up to stretch

Key Stage 2

WHAT YOU DO	WHAT YOU SAY
Ask them to perform the 'waves' = rock side to side on bottom (page 19)	• Show me our 'waves' movement • Now let's see if we can make it a bit more interesting. Can you do 4 rocks as they are, then another 4 rocks using your hand, elbow or arm as well?
Guide class through one or two developments together.	• Can those rocks make you move into another action? e.g., roll, spin, stretch. Or even two actions one after each other?
Encourage further developments where more than one movement response is possible	• Now you are going to do that whole phrase again and this time include – at least one part in slow motion – at least one part in fast forward • Now we are going to add those two versions together so you will have a much longer phrase. You will all finish at different times so when you get to the end just sit down and wait quietly for everyone to finish
Learn a partner's dance Join class together in pairs. Label A and B	You are going to teach your partner your dance First A is the teacher B is going to watch a do their dance once. Then A – you have to teach B your dance so that you can both do it at the same time. Make sure you tell them *how* to do the movements
Repeat the other way round Ask the pairs to join both dances together to make a longer dance	Now you have two parts to your dance- A's part and B's part. You can both dance both parts. You are going to join them together. You can decide in which order A – B or B – A

Key Stage 3

WHAT YOU DO	WHAT YOU SAY
Ask the pupils to perform actions 1-6 from the study all together. Ask them to choose two moments in that phrase to alter the speed and dynamics of the movement	At the moment you all have a phrase that looks the same. Now I want you to make some changes that make it *yours*. Choose two different moments in your phrase to alter the speed and dynamic so that it becomes more interesting. Try to surprise your audience. Don't choose the most obvious changes
Join them in pairs and learn part of their partner's phrase	Label yourselves A and B First, A is going to teach B your two changes so that you can both do them. Then B will teach A You now have an A version and a B version
They will join together A's and B's version, deciding where 'on stage' they will stand and face	You are both going to perform both versions, but you now have to decide how and where you will stand in relation to each other Is it possible to keep changing the direction each of you face? Can you sometimes face the same way and sometimes different ways? What effect does that create? Does it still suggest a waterfall?
Together, make final adjustments/ improvements to their duet	Now you are going to make your final improvements that will make your dance as exciting as possible for your audience. Do you both have to be moving all the time? If one moves, can the other respond somehow? Do you need to add in another movement to do that? Can you add in a surprise for your audience? Does your movement still suggest the shapes and qualities of a waterfall? Are you in time with your partner?

Your store cupboard of development ideas

Using just one or two of these ideas from the store cupboard makes quite a difference to the phrase. The idea is to get the pupils to make each phrase longer, rather than just changing one movement for another (see *Phrasing it right*, page 6). The more you use these methods, the more pupils will get used to them and automatically begin to think varying speed and level.

Changes   **Switches**   **Additions**   **Devices**

Enlargements   **Props**   **Repeats**

Changes

Change the speed of some or all of the phrase. See page 31

Change the direction (i.e. if going backwards, make some of it forwards) of some or all of the phase. See page 29

Change the rhythm of all or part of the phrase. See page 86

Change the pattern the dancers are making on the floor. e.g. if they are standing in a diagonal line – get them to move into a tightly spaced triangular formation. See page 29

Change the level of one or two movements. See page 30

Enlargements

If the original movement was just circling an arm backwards, then you 'enlarge' it by circling the arm, going up onto toes and then down so the circling arm can sweep the floor as well. See page 30

If the original movement was just with the foot, try moving the whole leg to have the same shape/ phrasing. See page 29

Switches

Switch the original body part for a different one. So if your original was circling an arm backwards, switch it to circling the hip or wrists, for example, very quickly three times.

If the original movement is on the horizontal plane, switch it to the vertical plane.

Props

Bring in props such as: hats, blocks, hoops, ribbons, sticks, chairs, and adapt the movement to combine with using the prop. See page 75

Use the props to suggest the beginnings of a story.

Additions

At any point in the phrase, just add in, for example, a jump, a roll and a turn. See page 30

Other additions may be: stillness, a sound made with the body, a surprise. See page 79

Additions

You can repeat a whole movement or just part of it. e.g. if circling repeat the first 180° of the circle four times before continuing

Repeat all or part of the phrase on the opposite side of the body

Repeat all or part of the phrase to a new direction. See page 63

Repeat all or part of the phrase with a different dynamic. See page 63

Devices

Here you perform the phrase in unison (like the Red Arrows flying together)

In canon (like a sung round)

With groups: mirroring each other or matching each other.

Performing and Appreciating

Performing

Dance is a performance art and as teachers we are trying to give pupils the opportunity to experience that sense (and hopefully enjoyment) of displaying something they have worked hard to produce. Showing work in a 'performance' situation creates a sense of occasion and adds status to the work they are doing. I believe it is a valuable experience for children to learn when their best effort is expected and that there are times when 'any old thing' won't do.

Many of the children we teach will enjoy movement and dance and only a few will make a living performing as dancers. Many will, however, gain much pleasure from participating in dance and other forms of movement as audience. We can help them inform that experience of watching so they are able to make judgements about what they see. This is called appreciating dance.

You should aim to include performance and observation/appreciation in every lesson in some form. At the simplest level, it may be two pupils showing each other their work in order to learn each other's dance or simply to copy movements. Or it may be a more formal situation of half the class watching the other half perform a dance followed by a questioning activity led by the teacher.

The teacher's role when guiding the class through the observation activity is to set one or two simple tasks to help the pupils to actually 'see' and therefore evaluate the movement.

Performance/appreciation at Key Stage 1

You are trying to help them look and 'see' something in particular about the movement. Give the children one specific thing to notice when watching, e.g. 'Watch you partner's dance and then tell/show me one wide shape that they made'. Or ' Watch your partner's dance and put your hand up when you see them jump'. They might make a simple judgement like 'Which shape did you like best? Why?'

Performance/appreciation at Key Stage 2

You are still trying to help them focus their viewing but now also encouraging them to make judgements about what they have seen, such as 'Watch your partner's dance and name three actions that they perform. Which one makes the most impact? Why' Or 'Watch your partner's dance and count how many times they make a wide shape. Could you suggest a way for them to perform one of those shapes on a different level? How would it be different/better?'

Performance/appreciation at Key Stage 3

You are still trying to focus their viewing but the emphasis is now on them making informed judgements about the work and decisions about what has or has not fulfilled the task, or what could be improved upon. You are aiming for it to become second nature for them to consider the movement they have produced, and not feel the need to accept everything they first think of as a final product. e.g. 'Watch your partner's dance and tell them one thing you really liked about it and why. Then tell them one thing you think they could improve and why.'

1. Working in pairs

Suitable for: Key Stage 1/Key Stage 2

Underlying idea

You begin by getting your pupils to observe others performing. From here you can move on to the skills needed to appreciate the performance.

What you do

Organise your class into pairs – label A and B

Tell the Bs to sit to the side of their partner, watching their A perform.

Reverse this afterwards

Step 1

What you say

- Watch your partner's dance and put up your hand when you see them jump

OR

- Watch your partner's dance and look for their low, wide shape. Be ready to show me the shape afterwards

Challenge tasks

- Name one other action they do apart from jumping
- Watch your partner's dance and tell me one other shape they make that is different

Step 2

What you say

- Watch your partner's dance and tell them one thing you really like about it. Then tell them one thing you think they could do better

Challenge tasks
- Make a suggestion to your partner about what they might do to improve that bit you thought they could do better. Tell them or show them

Suitable for: Key Stage 3

What you do
Ask them to find a partner. Label themselves A and B and sit down in a space.
What you say
- You are going to watch each other perform and look for [whatever is the lesson objective]. As first, then Bs

Step 1

- Watch your partner's dance and name three different actions they use e.g. turn, roll, stamp, jump

OR

- Watch your partner's dance and look for three movements that clearly show 'Anger'. Tell them why afterwards

Step 2

- Watch your partner's dance and tell them one thing that clearly answers the set task. Say why. Then tell them one thing that still needs improvement before it does answer the task. Say why

Challenge task
- Watch your partner's dance then learn it so that you can perform it with them

2. Working larger groups/half class observation

Suitable for: Key Stage 2

Underlying idea
You begin by getting your pupils to observe others performing. From here you can move on to the skills needed to appreciate the performance.

What you do
Divide the class in half. One half moves to the side of the room to observe the other half perform.
Reverse this later.
Ask them to pick one person/group to observe (you may set this yourself).

Step 1

What you say
* Can you name three different things they do (e.g. jump, turn, roll, stamp, etc)
OR
* Can you tell me one action e.g. jump, turn, roll, stamp, etc that they do the same as you; and one action e.g. jump, turn, roll, stamp etc, that they do differently from you
OR
* Name two levels that person uses. Do they use any more than once?

Step 2

* Watch one person/group and make a mental note of whether they have included all the things asked for in the task (remind the class what these were at this point)
OR
* Watch one person/group and choose one idea of theirs to include in your dance which you think answers the task well
(remind the class of the task again at this point)
OR
* Name two levels that person uses. Do they use any more than once?

Challenge tasks
* Watch one person/group and then be ready to demonstrate one movement or part of the dance that you particularly liked and explain why.

Cool down

Cooling down is about gradually slowing down the circulation of the blood in order to return to a resting heart rate. This final section of the lesson has three purposes.

Firstly, it is important not to stop exercising suddenly. It must be reduced gradually otherwise blood can pool in areas of the body that have been very active causing soreness or even dizziness and fainting. Gentle stretching and breathing activities are most effective to bring the heart rate back to normal.

Secondly, this time is also useful for bringing the whole class together before the lesson finishes to help to consolidate the material learnt in the lesson. You may pose simple questions to the class while they are holding a few simple stretches.

Thirdly, it is also a very useful way to calm a class down (particularly if they have had a very lively lesson) and prepare them to go back to the classroom. Some nice deep breaths are always good for this one. Stretches done sitting or even lying down are most effective for an over-excited class.

The cool down needs to be something very simple and led by the teacher. If you don't feel confident standing out in front of the class gather them into a circle (see class organisation ideas in the Warm up section) so that all your pupils can join in easily and quietly. Try repeating an idea from earlier in the lesson but much slower and with pauses to emphasise moments of stretch. Or as a complete contrast to the lesson's contents do something very different. It can even be something as simple as walking in a figure of eight and making different wide shapes when they have finished. Then sit them down in a position that stretches the legs and lead a short question and answer session on the work covered in that lesson.

Cool down 1

What you do	What you say	Look out for/notes
Class stand facing the teacher	Make the biggest/widest shape you can think of	Encourage the stretch right to the end of the fingers and toes
	Make the smallest/narrowest shape you can think of	Encourage them to breathe in deeply on the stretch and breathe out on the turn into small shape
	Join them together using a slow turning movement	
	Repeat three times	

Especially useful for younger pupils. This might be an activity you do at the end of each lesson.

Cool down 2

What you do	What you say	Look out for/notes
Get them to stand side by side with a partner	Make a wide symmetrical shape (so yo are like a mirror image of your partner)	Encourage maximum stretch through the whole body
	Make a wide asymmetrical shape (so you are different from your partner)	Encourage deep breath in on held shapes and slow breath out on turn
	Join them together using a slow turning movement	Symmetry and asymmetry need to be terms they already
	Repeat three times	

Especially useful for Key Stage 3 to consolidate earlier work on shape or symmetry/asymmetry

Cool down 3

What you do	What you say	Look out for/notes
Get them to work individually	Hold three shapes you have used during the lesson for two deep breaths each Can you stretch further in those shapes Can you change the shape slightly so you feel the stretch in a different part of the body?	Encourage them to stretch to the maximum Be careful about wobbles, they may need to support themselves against a wall to avoid falling over

Especially useful when you want to consolidate work from earlier in the lesson

Cool down 4

What you do	What you say	Look out for/notes
Get them to lie on the floor with their arms by their sides Repeat this three times. Then ask them to relax	Breathe in and stretch your arms above your head, point your toes Hold your breath for a count of three Slowly breath out and let your arms go back to where they started and push heels away to stretch back of legs Now let everything relax and just enjoy a moment of complete rest.	Encourage them not to arch their backs as they lift the arms – use tummy muscles to keep their back flat Encourage smooth exhalation This MUST be in silence

Conclusion

A successful lesson should end with you as teacher reminding the class of the lesson objectives and how they were achieved.

Gather the class nearer in to you so you don't have to shout, and ask questions such as:

- 'What have we been working on today?'
- ' What does that mean?'
- 'What was out starting point today?'
- 'Can you think of a new movement you have tried today?'
- 'What is a symmetrical/asymmetrical shape?'

Always aim to finish the lesson on a positive note. Be generous with praise individually and collectively. If you have a reward system use it here. Aim to motivate the children to look forward to their next dance lesson with you.

Units of Work
Introduction

Although these units of work have been assigned to particular Key Stage groups, **they can be adapted to work with any age group**, given some of the guidelines earlier in the book.

Feel free to adapt and develop. These are guidelines only – set out so that you can put together dance lessons that are valuable and that work. Once you're used to working with them, then you'll get a feel for the way to adapt each unit most appropriately for different age/ability groups.

Key Stage One

1. Maori Legend

(3 hours)

Creating movement from text

This unit of work takes a Maori legend as the starting point. Some background work could be done on who the Maoris are, their history and customs. It would also be an ideal unit to combine with mask making. Some of the pupils will know of the *haka* performed by the New Zealand All Blacks rugby team before they play. Use this to give them the feel of traditional Maori dance. Maybe even have a go. There is no necessity to use authentic Maori movements in this unit, but it could be an interesting way in. The important thing is to encourage a movement response that is fuller than simply miming the words. Think of the words as a springboard to 'launch' the movement. This is called abstraction.

Resources
* the legend (included in this unit)
* tape/CD player if wish to use music
* pictures/photographs of Maoris in traditional dress (not essential)

Where the unit fits in
This unit lays the foundations for future units, in which children will explore a wider range of dance. They will look at how different body actions show moods and feelings, and will learn to use different parts of the body to lead movements. They will use language associated with movement to evaluate and improve their dances.

Prior Learning
It is helpful if the children have
* followed simple instructions
* moved using simple rhythms
* explored basic body actions
* watched and talked about movement
* had some experience of action songs and rhymes

Learning Objectives
* To explore movement ideas and respond imaginatively to given stimuli
* To move confidently and safely in their own and general space, using changes of speed, level and direction
* To compose and link movement phrases to make simple dances, with clear beginnings, middles and ends
* To perform movement phrases using a range of body actions and body parts
* To talk about dance ideas inspired by different stimuli
* To copy, watch and describe dance movement

Maori Legend

How Maui Caught The Sun

For the purposes of this unit the story has been split into sections.

Maui is a character from Maori mythology. His father was Makea-tu-tara, a god and his mother was an earth woman Taranga. According to legend Maui was born prematurely and thus abandoned – which was the custom of the time. A divine ancestor intervened and raised him, educating him in magical lore. Eventually Maui returned to his family and became his mother's favourite son. He was always curious and was often up to mischief, usually ending up in trouble. Murriranga, his ancestress, gave him the gift of a magic jawbone which he used frequently, but not always wisely!

For the purposes of this unit the story has been split into sections.

Section 1

When Maui was a young man, the sun travelled *quickly across the sky* each day so that the days were very short. This was a problem because there was *not enough time* to do all the things that had to be done. *Not enough time* for the men to catch fish. *Not enough time* for the women to weave the flax to make clothes. *Not enough time* to grow things in the

garden. There was **not even enough time** for the children to play. What could be done? Maui's brothers came to him and asked him to help them with his magic.

Maui made a plan – he would **trap the sun** in a big net, beat it with his magic stick and make it slow down. Then the days would be longer. Maui's brothers were frightened. They said, "**The sun is too hot**. It will burn us with its rays". But eventually Maui persuaded them to help him work the flax to make long ropes which were very strong.

When all was ready they travelled far to find the big hole through which the sun rose by the sea. "We will **trap the sun,**" they whispered. They set their trap to catch the sun and waited.

Section 2

"We must make a **place to hide,**" said Maui or the sun will see us and our plan will fail. He told his brothers to make a house from the branches of a large tree. "We will **hide** in the house and the sun will not see us," he said. The brothers worked hard and built the house and indeed Maui and his brothers were all able to **hide behind its walls.**

At sunrise, the sun's head and shoulders pushed through the hole and he **peeked over the edge of the world** to see if night had gone. He did not see Maui and his brothers hiding and he did not see the long flax ropes. The sun climbed steadily higher and higher, ready to go **rushing across the sky.**

"**Wait,**" said Maui. "**Keep absolutely still.**" They could all see clearly the **huge, round, yellow face** of the sun and his golden eyes. **"Wait,"** said Maui. **"Keep absolutely still**". They could feel the warm heat of his breath on their faces. The sun's head came nearer and nearer to the net. **"Wait,"** said Maui. The sun stood in front of them **like an enormous giant.** His head was nearly inside the net. **"Wait,"** said Maui.

Section 3

The sun's **head rose right into the net**. "Now !" shouted Maui and the brothers pulled the net as tight as they could. The strong ropes **trapped his arms**. They **tripped up his legs**. The ropes **wound round and round** the sun so that he could **no longer easily move**. "What trick is this?" screeched the sun. He **pulled and screamed** and **twisted and turned** but Maui and his brothers held on tight. Maui beat the sun with his magic stick until he was too **weary, weak and frightened** to fight anymore.

"Stop! Please let me go!" cried the sun. "You have defeated me. What is it that you wish?" "You are **running too fast over the sky** each day," said Maui "Our days are too short." "I'm sorry," said the sun, **shaking with fear**. "I promise I will slow down if you will just set me free."
Maui agreed and told his brothers to untie the ropes which **fell away to the ground**. The sun **shuddered** and **limped slowly** into the sky.

And from then on, the sun has ***travelled slowly and painfully*** across the heavens each day

Section 4

When Maui and his brothers returned home the people of the land were very happy. The days were longer. There was ***plenty of time*** to catch fish. ***Plenty of time*** to grow things in the garden. ***Plenty of time*** to work the flax. ***Plenty of time*** for the children to play. And of course, ***plenty of time*** for Maui and his brothers to tell the story of how clever they had been in catching the sun!

THE END

Firstly read the whole story to the class. This does not necessarily need to be done in the dance lesson time.

Section 1
Task 1

Read again the italicised words to the class. For each ask them to suggest a movement or movements which visually suggest the words. Remember you are not looking for them to mime. Encourage them to use something from the words as a 'springboard' for fuller movement.

e.g.	*quickly across the sky*	= circle right arm backwards twice then crouch to floor,
	not enough time	= stand feet apart, arms crossed in front of body
	trap the sun	= jump high, circle arm inwards **and** push down (as if catching sun **and** pushing into the ground)
	the sun is too hot	= sit on the floor tap soles of feet quickly on floor drum fingers on floor

If a pupil comes up with a good idea, then get everyone to try it.

Task 2

From the ideas they have tried, decide with the pupils on a movement phrase for each italicised phrase.
Teacher reads story and pupils all perform movements as the words are read out.
Movement phrases may well take longer than the words so pause the reading where necessary.

Group work

Arrange the class into small groups of two, three or four.
Can you organise yourselves into an interesting group shape to perform the movement phrases we have practised? You may need to alter the movement slightly.

Challenge task
The movements could be developed further as follows:

1st phrase = each child use a different speed
2nd phrase = each child use a different level
3rd phrase = each child face a different direction
4th phrase = all be different sizes

Task 3

Set the different groups in various places in the performing space and read through the whole section with movements.

Note:
It would be quite enough to have the story read alone, but other alternatives might be:

*   have quiet music played during the story
*   have groups of pupils saying different parts of the story
*   have pupils using basic percussion in addition to the music
*   have the story read, followed by pupils singing a song while dancing

Section 2
Task 4

Read the italicised words and explain that you are going to use them in a similar way to section one but this time aim to make longer phrases of movement.
Ask them which words may suggest moving in a particular way:

e.g.   *quickly across the sky*   suggests moving quickly following a slightly curved pathway
   hide suggests something/ someone being partly covered by something/ someone
   i.e. pupil A's arm covers B's shoulder
   keep absolutely still suggests holding an interesting shape in stillness

Group work

*   Arrange class into different groups of three from the last section
*   Allocate one phrase to each group

PHRASE A
*   Make a still picture to suggest something in the words
*   Develop the movement by adding an action word before the picture and after the picture, e.g. roll, jump, slide, travel, drop, lift
*   They now have a longer movement phrase e.g. PHRASE A = roll > picture > slide

Task 5

PHRASE B
Make a second picture to suggest something else from the words. Try to make it very different from the first one.
Encourage each pupils to use a different level and size movement from their Phrase A.

Link the second picture to the sequence so far and follow with another action word.
Finish the sequence with a final still picture (this could be a new one or one of the two previous pictures).

Link it all together to make one long phrase of movement performed by the whole group.
e.g. ACTION > PICTURE 1 > ACTION > ACTION > PICTURE 2 > ACTION > FINAL PICTURE.

Challenge task
 Arrange your phrase to include at least two different speeds and to face two different directions
Do you all have to do the same movement at the same time?

Observation task
*   Watch one group perform their sequence.
*   Can you identify two different actions?
*   Can you guess the words they used as a starting point? Which movements suggest this?

Task 6

Arrange the groups in the space and then an order for the groups to perform their sequences one after the other.

Read Section 2 as the accompaniment. Pause where you need to.

Note:
The movement phrases do not have to be performed as the relevant lines are read.

If you have more able pupils they may also be able to learn another group's phrase as well as their own. This will then give you the scope to perform them either in unison or canon.

Section 3
Task 7

*   Organise the class into different groups of three or four. (This is their 3rd group.)
*   You are going to repeat the process for Section 2

Read the italicised words and explain that you are going to use them in a similar way to Section 2.

Ask them which words may suggest moving in a particular way:
e.g.
*   *wound round and round* suggests one body part moving around another
and closing in
*   *tripped* suggests sudden, light movement slightly out of control
*   *shaking with fear* suggests shaking body parts separately and/ or together

Group work

PHRASE A
*   Arrange the class into different groups of three from last section
*   Allocate a phrase to each group
*   Make a still picture to suggest something in the words
*   Develop the movement by adding an action word before the picture and after the picture e.g. roll, jump, slide, travel drop, lift
They now have a longer movement phrase e.g. PHRASE A = roll > picture > slide

Task 8

PHRASE B
*   Make a second picture to suggest something else from the words. Try to make it very different to the first one
*   Encourage each pupil to use a different level and size movement to their Phrase A

Link the second picture to the sequence so far and follow with another action word.
Finish the sequence with a final still picture (this could be a new one or one of the two previous pictures).

Task 9

Link it all together to make one long phrase of movement performed by the whole group.
e.g. ACTION > PICTURE 1 > ACTION > ACTION > PICTURE 2 > ACTION > FINAL PICTURE.

Challenge task
*   Arrange your phrase to include at least two different levels and to face two different directions
*   Do you all have to do the same movement at the same time?

Observation task
Watch one group perform their sequence
*   Can you identify two different actions?
*   Can you guess the words they used as a starting point? Which movements suggest this?

Task 10

Arrange the groups in the space and then an order for the groups to perform their sequences one after the other.

Read Section 3 as the accompaniment. Pause where necessary.

Note:
The movement phrases do not have to be performed as the relevant lines are read.

If you have more able pupils they may also be able to learn another group's phrase as well as their own. This will then give you the scope to perform them either in unison or canon.

Section 4
Task 11

Organise the class into their 4th group.
You are going to repeat the process for Section 1.

Read again the italicised words to the class. For each ask them to suggest a movement or movements which visually make a suggestion of the words. Remember you are not looking for them to mime. Encourage them to use something from the words as a 'springboard' for fuller movement.

e.g.
*   *were very happy* – open, uplifted movements, smiling
*   *was plenty of time* – turn on spot into standing feet apart arms open in wide V shape
    –- at a different level on each repetition

Task 12

From the ideas they have tried, decide with the pupils on a movement phrase for each italicised phrase.

Teacher reads the story and pupils all perform movements as the words are read out. Movement phrases may well take longer than the words so pause the reading where necessary.

Group work

Can you organise yourselves into an interesting group shape to perform the movement phrases we have practised? You may need to alter the movement slightly.

Challenge task

The movements could be developed further as follows:

1st phrase: each child use a different speed
2nd phrase: each child use a different level
3rd phrase: each child face a different direction
4th phrase: all be different sizes

Set the different groups in various places in the performing space and read through the whole section with movements.

At the end of the unit all the sections can be put together and performed as a class dance.

DANCE STRUCTURE

SECTION 1 SEQUENCE (GROUP 1) > WALK TO NEXT GROUP > SECTION 2 SEQUENCE (GROUP 2) > WALK TO NEXT GROUP > SECTION 3 SEQUENCE (GROUP 3) > WALK TO NEXT GROUP > SECTION 4 SEQUENCE (GROUP 4)

Learning Outcomes

PERFORMANCE   copy and explore basic body actions demonstrated by the teacher
copy simple movement patterns from each other and explore the movement
practise and repeat their movement phrases and perform them in a controlled way

COMPOSITION   choose movements to make into their own phrases with beginnings, middles and ends

APPRECIATION   use simple dance vocabulary to describe movement

HEALTH AND SAFETY

- Are the children wearing footwear and clothing that are safe and help their learning?
- Is the space safe and clear enough to work in?
- Are the children aware of others in the class when they are moving around?
- Have all the children warmed up and cooled down properly?

Expectations

When carrying out the type of activities and tasks in this unit

Most children will be able to: perform basic body actions, use different parts of the body singly and in combination; show some sense of dynamic, expressive and rhythmic qualities in their own dance; choose appropriate movements for different dance ideas; remember and repeat short dance phrases and simple dances; move with control; vary the way they use space; describe basic body actions and simple expressive and dynamic qualities of movement

Some children will not have made so much progress. They will be able to: explore basic body actions; begin to make single movements and combine movements using different parts of the body; practise moving clearly and expressively; try to choose movements that reflect the dance idea; with help, remember, repeat and link movement phrases; recognise and describe some body actions and some expressive and dynamic qualities of movement
Perform different body actions, use different parts of the body singly and in combination

Some children will have progressed further. They will be able to: perform more complicated combinations of movement fluently and with control; perform clearly and expressively; choose movements that show a clear understanding of the dance idea; talk about dance using a range of descriptive language

2. Pancakes

(3 hours)

This unit encourages children to have fun with movement, and experiment with different body shapes and ways of moving. Children explore basic body shapes e.g. rounded or angular, big or small, and use different parts of their body to make movements. They create and repeat short dances based on the stimulus.

Resources

Percussion instruments, e.g. tambourine, sticks

Prior Learning

It is helpful if the children have
* followed simple instructions
* explored a range of body actions
* created and copied a short movement phrase
* had some experience of watching dance and describing body actions

Where the unit fits in

In this unit children focus on creating and performing short dances that communicate an idea. They will look at how different body actions show moods and feelings, and will learn to use different parts of the body to lead movements. They will use language associated with movement to evaluate and improve their dances.

Learning Objectives

* To explore movement ideas and respond imaginatively to given stimuli
* To move confidently and safely in their own and general space, using changes of speed, level and direction
* To compose and link movement phrases to make simple dances, varying simple compositional ideas
* To explore, remember, repeat and link a range of actions with coordination, control and an awareness of the expressive qualities of dance
* To watch and describe dance phrases and use what they learn to improve their own work

Pancake ingredients

Discuss the making of pancakes. e.g. What ingredients? The sequence of adding the ingredients?

Task 1

When experimenting with ideas – start with 'egg'

EGG

Make a large rounded shape. Do you have to be standing on your feet?
Make a different rounded shape. Choose which one you like best.
Perform the shapes half a class at a time.

Performance task

Can you really curve your body so that there are no straight lines or angles anywhere?

Observation task

Which is the most interesting rounded shape you can see? Why? Who has made the best job of being totally rounded with their body?

Give image of egg being cracked open

Encourage a fast, sudden, angular movement.
Create jagged edges with elbow, knees, hands, hips, heels.
Try three or four different shapes and pick the two you like best.
Perform with a beat of sticks as accompaniment.

FLOUR

Give image of sifting flour into the bowl.
Sifting = shaking.
Teacher leads the class making a shake through the whole body.
e.g. start with right foot only – whole right leg – hips only – ribs only – shoulders only – whole body.

Challenge task

- Could the shaking lead you into another movement at the same time e.g. turning, jumping, spiral down

Performance task

- Try to make your movements as loose and floppy as you can (complete contrast to the cracked egg shapes)
- Can you vary the strength and size of the shakes as they reach different parts of your body? e.g. small and gentle, large and strong
- Find a still position to finish – try to make it a sudden freeze frame of a shaking action (as if the teacher takes a photograph of the last shaking action)

MILK

Discuss descriptive words for milk pouring into the bowl. Use the suggested words to give ideas for movement, i.e. splosh, splash could be heavy, loose and floppy movements with

hands and feet.
(Pupils can provide their own accompaniment with their voices to this movement).

Group work

In groups of three, each choose an ingredient.
Make the pancake: flour + egg + milk by each child performing their ingredient.
When the milk has 'poured', all the ingredients swirl and spiral, then all make a pancake shape (one large or individual) as though poured into frying pan.

Challenge task
* Teach each other your egg, flour and milk phrases
* Each child performs all three ideas for each ingredient

PANCAKE COOKING

Give image of heat coming from below and the little bubbles that appear in the batter mixture.
Use lots of different quick and small movements with different parts of the body rising away from the floor
e.g. elbow, knee, hand, shoulder, heel.

Tossing   Slowly move to a crouch, and jump to face different direction.

Rolling   On own or in group — forwards, backwards, sideways

Being eaten   Gradually draw in body as pancake is eaten

Final shape   Make a funny still picture on your own that tells me you've eaten too many
                   pancakes.

Don't forget to use facial expression.

DANCE STRUCTURE

EGG > FLOUR > MILK > PANCAKE SHAPE > COOKING > TOSSING > ROLLING >
BEING EATEN > FINAL SHAPE

Work on linking these sections together smoothly. Where does one phrase end and the other begin?

NB: If making one large pancake work on group shape, spacing, direction children are facing.

Observation task
Watch a group perform their dance. Can you pick out
One egg movement.
One milk movement.
One cooking movement.

Learning Outcomes

PERFORMANCE	copy and explore basic body actions demonstrated by the teacher
	copy simple movement patterns from each other and explore the movement
	perform short dances using rhythmic and dynamic qualities to express ideas and feelings
COMPOSITION	choose and link movements to make short dance phrases that express an idea or feeling
	talk about different stimuli as the starting point for creating dance
	explore actions in response to stimuli
APPRECIATION	describe dance phrases and expressive qualities
	say what they like and dislike, giving reasons

HEALTH AND SAFETY

- Are the children wearing footwear and clothing that are safe and help their learning?
- Is the space safe and clear enough to work in?
- Are the children aware of others in the class when they are moving around?
- Have all the children warmed up and cooled down properly?

Expectations

When carrying out the type of activities and tasks in this unit

Most children will be able to: perform basic body actions, use different parts of the body singly and in combination; show some sense of dynamic, expressive and rhythmic qualities in their own dance; choose appropriate movements for different dance ideas; remember and repeat short dance phrases and simple dances; move with control; vary the way they use space; describe basic body actions and simple expressive and dynamic qualities of movement.

Some children will not have made so much progress. They will be able to: explore basic body actions; begin to make single movements and combine movements using different parts of the body; practise moving clearly and expressively; try to choose movements that reflect the dance idea; with help, remember, repeat and link movement phrases; recognise and describe some body actions and some expressive and dynamic qualities of movement.

Some children will have progressed further: They will be able to: perform more complicated combinations of movement fluently and with control; perform clearly and expressively; choose movements that show a clear understanding of the dance idea; talk about dance using a range of descriptive language.

Key Stage Two

3. Action words

(4-5 hours)

In this unit children perform dances, focusing on creating, adapting and linking a range of dance actions from a purely movement based starting point. This can be less threatening for pupils without much dance experience than trying to interpret an idea or theme. The action words link to make a **motif** which can then be **developed.** They work individually and in pairs. I have included some pages (pages 67-74) with different examples of words which you can then enlarge and laminate or put onto OHPs. You could set the words as an art task and make big words on the wall. You could also use this section in work on literacy.

Resources
- a cassette or CD player
- a white/blackboard or action cards/OHPs/laminates etc

Prior Learning
It is helpful if children have:
- structured short dance phrases and dances on their own and with a partner
- used a range of descriptive language for dance
- talked to each other about dance and listened to each other describing dance

Where the unit fits in
This unit lays the foundations for Unit 4 *Seasons* in which children will concentrate on dance inspired by visual stimuli. They will continue to work on their own, with a partner and in small groups, developing their ability to create, perform and appreciate dance.

Learning Objectives
- To improvise freely on their own and with a partner, translating ideas from language to movement
- To create and link dance phrases using a simple dance structure or motif
- To perform dances with an awareness of rhythmic, dynamic and expressive qualities, on their own and with a partner.
- To describe some of the compositional features of dances
- To talk about how they might improve their dances

Actions

Task 1

This first task should be performed individually.

Teacher writes the following 'action words' on the board or on cards.

(Large format versions of these words for photocopying begin on page 67. Other examples of words are given on pages 75-77.)

Run   Spin   Wave   Walk   Jump   Roll   Drop   Crawl

Discuss each word with the class, and its different movement possibilities. Encourage individual pupils to suggest movements for each word and allow the rest of the class to try them. Encourage pupils to try one large and one small movement for each action.

e.g. *Drop*
- could start from standing and drop whole body to crouch position
- could start with arm high and drop arm heavily to side
- could begin kneeling and drop chin towards chest

Crawl
- could crawl on hands and knees on floor
- could sit in tucked shape and crawl fingers down one leg

Encourage pupils to think of an action word for a) whole body and b) individual body parts. (The latter often gets more interesting results.)

Motif

Task 2

- Pick three of the action words to create a simple phrase of movement. Pupils should be able to repeat the phrase. This is called a MOTIF.
- Experiment with different word orders to see which works best.
- Include at least one large and one small shape in your phrase.

Development

When you are happy with your motif see if you can make it more interesting by:
- changing direction suddenly
- changing its dynamics/energy

e.g.	**Spin**	**Fall**	**Wave**
	very slowly	**suddenly**	**frantically**

- changing level
- adding or repeating an action

- changing the size of an action. Experiment with making big movements smaller and vice versa

Challenge task
- Can you think of some movements which are asymmetric and 'off balance' to include? This will encourage pupils to move their bodies in new and unfamiliar ways to produce movements that are more exciting than symmetrical 'safe' movements

Pair work

Task 3

- Organise class into pairs
- Teach each other your motifs so that both pupils can perform both motifs. Label them Motif A and Motif B
- When teaching your motif to your partner pay particular attention to *how* you want the different movements performed. e.g. the kick is performed suddenly and strongly to the right leading with the heel

Observation task
- Watch your partner perform your motif
- Tell them which bits they are performing well and which bits need more work
- Try to give them one piece of advice to improve their performance
  e.g. look up at the clock on the wall to keep focus high

Task 4

Each person should now have learnt their partner's phrase and be able to perform it using the same speeds, levels, sizes and dynamics. Suddenly they will have a much wider range of movement vocabulary. This is also a useful exercise as it trains the pupil to communicate their ideas clearly and develops their movement memory.

Challenge task
The 'motif' and 'development' section could be repeated two or three times to make longer movement phrases.
Each pair then organises their movement material as they wish to make a short dance.

DANCE STRUCTURE

Example 1: MOTIF A (BOTH PUPILS IN UNISON) > MOTIF B (PUPIL 2) > MOTIF B (PUPIL 1) > MOTIF A (IN CANON)

Example 2: MOTIF B (CANON) > MOTIF A (CANON) > MOTIF A & B (TOGETHER) > MOTIF A (UNISON)

Group work

If the pupils have responded well to the pair work it could be developed further by organising pairs to join to make groups of four. The pairs could then repeat the process of teaching each other their dances, and join them together to make a longer dance.

Learning Outcomes

PERFORMANCE   show an imaginative response to language through their choice of movement
incorporate different qualities and dynamics into their movement
perform short dances with expression, showing an awareness of others when moving

COMPOSITION   link actions to make dance phrases, working with a partner and small groups

APPRECIATION   describe what makes a good dance phrase
use a range of expressive language to describe dance
recognise unison and canon and suggest improvements

HEALTH AND SAFETY
- Are the children wearing footwear and clothing that are safe and help their learning?
- Is the space safe and clear enough to work in?
- Are the children aware of others on the class when they are moving around?
- Have all the children warmed up and cooled down properly?

Expectations

When carrying out the type of activities and tasks in this unit

Most children will be able to: improvise freely, translating ideas from a stimulus into movement; share and create dance phrases with a partner and in a small group; repeat, remember and perform these phrases in a dance; use dynamic, rhythmic and expressive qualities clearly and with control; understand the importance of warming up and cooling down; recognise and talk about the movements used and the expressive qualities of dance; suggest improvements to their own and other people's dances.

Some children will not have made so much progress. They will be able to: demonstrate some basic skills; perform movements with control; try to show a sense of dynamics and expressive qualities when dancing; contribute basic ideas to the structure of a dance; come up with basic responses to a stimulus; show some understanding of why they need to warm up and cool down; use simple words to describe and interpret dance.

Some children will have progressed further. They will be able to: use a wide range of movements when improvising; take the lead when creating dances with a partner or in a group; show greater understanding of how to create dance phrases; show greater fluency and control in their movements; interpret rhythm well; interpret and express their thoughts clearly when talking about dance; make appropriate suggestions about how work could be improved.

Sample action words for use in group work follow on pages 67 to 74.

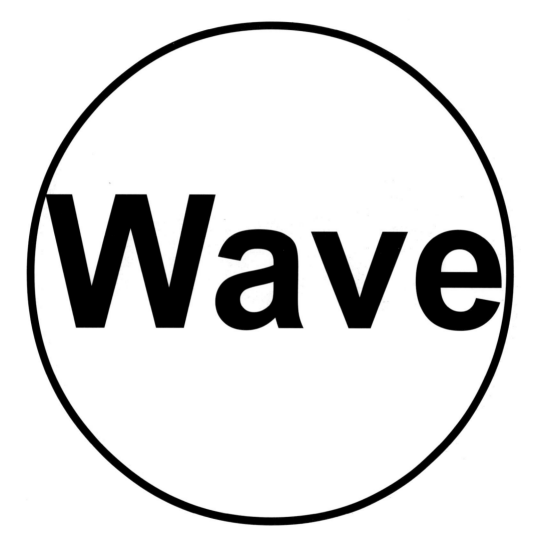

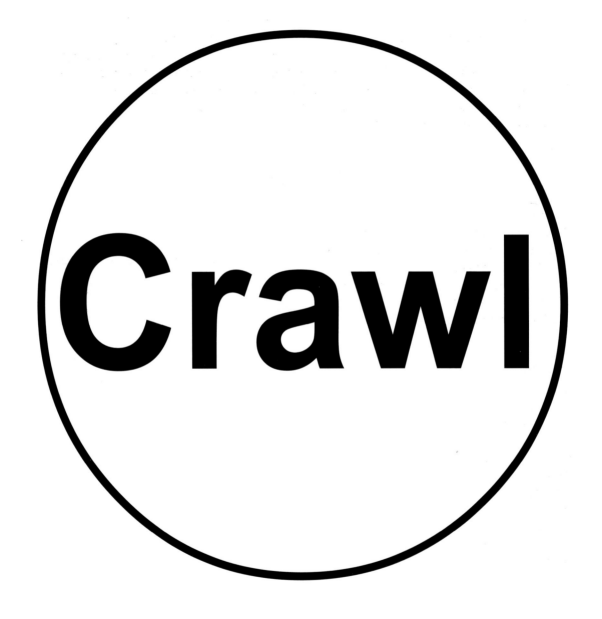

Sample ideas for specific National Curriculum themes

Listed below are ideas for Pirates, Egyptians, Victorians and Electricity. There are three headings for each: **action**, **shapes** and **props/costume**. You can use any or all of these words in place of the 'action words' in the unit above.

For example: if your theme is Pirates, think of **actions** a pirate may do – WALK the plank, JUMP over another pirate's sword (in a fight), SALUTE the captain, PULL the rope to raise the pirate flag. You may even extend the idea to include **shapes** associated with the subject – in this case SWORD, CROSS AND BONE, SAILS, X(marks the spot on a treasure map). These shapes can be substituted for the action words and the scheme followed in exactly the same way. **Props** or items of **costume** often give children new ideas for movement and allow them to get deeper into the movement.

PIRATES

Actions
WALK (the plank)
JUMP (over another pirate's sword in fight)
SALUTE the captain
PULL/HEAVE the ropes to raise the flag
POINT to the treasure
WOBBLE when drunk

Shapes
SWORD
SAIL
CROSS AND BONE
X (marks the spot)

Props/costume
EYE PATCH
SWORD
DAGGER
FLAG
TREASURE MAP
HAT

VICTORIANS

Actions
REACH (up to clean the chimney)
STILLNESS (sitting in the classroom)
GALLOP (horses for transport)
WALK (to school)
SHAKE (out the washing)

Shapes
CHIMNEY BROOM
HORSES CART
CHALK & SLATE
THE CANE

Props/costume
LONG DRESSES
SHAWLS
KNEE BRITCHES
WAISTCOATS
CAPS
CANES

EGYPTIANS

Actions
WALK (elbows bent, palms of hands facing up)
LUNGE (forwards with heavy stone on backs for building pyramid)
LIFT   (water from the rivers/canals)
THROW (spears and lines for fishing)
PULL (oxen pulling ploughs)

Shapes
PYRAMID
PHARAOH HEAD
HIEROGLYPHICS
MUMMIES

Props/costume
RICH GOLD FABRIC
BANDAGES
SHADOOF(water carrier)

FISHING NETS
JEWELLERY

ELECTRICITY

Actions
LEAP (lightening flash through sky)
SHAKE (the current)
JUMP (energy boost from a transformer)
CIRCLE (a circuit)
SPIRAL (wire coil in generators)

Shapes
WIRES/CABLES
BATTERIES
LIGHTNING FLASH
LIGHT BULB
PYLONS
+ - SIGNS

Props/costume
COLOURED SASH/RIBBON (wires)
2 COLOUR BALLOONS, MASKS OR T-SHIRTS (to represent positive and negative)
ROPE (to make a circuit)

4. Seasons

(4 hours)

This unit takes the 'Action Word' idea one stage further by the addition of a stimulus from nature. Pictures, photographs or paintings of autumn and/or winter scenes could provide a useful way into discussion of how seasons change. In this unit children focus on dancing with other people. They create, perform and watch dances working individually and in large groups.

Resources

- tape or CD player
- white/blackboard or action cards
- pictures, photographs or paintings of autumn/winter scenes

Prior Learning

It is helpful if children have:
- created and performed simple dances in groups
- used video and/or other visual images to create initial ideas
- gained experience of talking about dance, art and music
- gained experience of talking about how to improve their compositions and performances

Where the unit fits in

This unit provides the opportunity for children to use different visual images as a starting point for dance. They will be encouraged to become more adventurous when improvising and exploring ideas; developing their ability to work in a group. In other physical education units in Year 5 children concentrate on designing and creating complex group sequences using music (gymnastics) and exploring pattern and space (games).

Learning Objectives

- to explore and improvise ideas for dances using a variety of dance actions in response to a given stimulus
- to compose dances by using, adapting and developing a variety of actions, formations and patterns
- to perform dances expressively, using a range of performance skills
- to describe, analyse, and evaluate dances, showing an understanding of the interpretation of a stimulus

Autumn

Talk about how seasons change.

What images do you have of summer changing into autumn?
* colour changes from greens to reds/browns
* leaves falling from trees
* wind swirling leaves
* bright sunny days but chilly
* wrap up in woolly scarves

Think more closely about the idea of leaves. What words describe them?

Swirling   twirling   sway   dip   rustle   spin   spiral   float   drop

Task 1
* Place a collection of cards face down on the floor. All cards have a word written on them

Or

* Write the words on a black/whiteboard

LEAF SEQUENCE
* Go through each word with the class first –- finding movements for each
* Each child then takes three cards/ picks three words from the board which give them three actions to perform
* Each child makes a sequence using each word at least once and any word up to twice
* Say the word as you do it - in the manner in which it is performed, e.g 'Rustle' = hiss the s sound
* 'Float' – elongate the oa sound
* 'Drop' – sudden, quick – pop the p sound

Performance task
* Can you exaggerate the contrast in the qualities of the movement?
  e.g. float – high, lifted and light – almost weightless
* drop – fast heavy, sudden
* spiral – high to low, big to small, fast to slow

* Can you make the different shapes of your body very clear as you are moving?
  e.g. stretched, curled, one hand lifted, looking at elbow

Observation task
* In pairs
* Watch your partner perform their sequence

- Can you identify three body shapes they use?
- Can you identify two different dynamics they use?
- Can you identify two different levels they use?
- Which movement has the most impact on you? Why?

Firstly, partners feed back on all these questions to each other.
Secondly, the teacher asks whole class to suggest examples of each from those they watched – pick three or four for each and ask the pupils to demonstrate.

Perhaps try out some of the examples with the whole class.

Give the pupils one final opportunity to practise and improve their sequence – speed, energy, clarity, held positions.

Challenge task
- Add in one or two new movements you have learnt from the performance and observation tasks to make a longer sequence

Task 2

- Spread the class out in the room and each find a starting position

- Pick a leader to begin his/her sequence and others join in as they wish in canon (while saying the words perform the action)
- All hold the last position

Task 3

BUILDING A BONFIRE
When the last one finishes, the leader again starts off the process and all make way to the centre of the room to make a large structure. To do this each child picks another card/ action to give a method of travelling to the centre.

Build up one body shape on another – image of leaves in a big heap – to make a bonfire.

Encourage pupils to be at different heights, face different directions and have different parts of the body sticking out of the fire e.g. elbows, knees, hips, bottom, head.

FIRE BUILDING UP
- When the last one is in place, someone at the bottom makes sound and movement to start the 'fire'
- Only very small at first, e.g. drumming fingers on floor
- Gradually sparks catch to other leaves and fire grows e.g. slap hands on legs, thighs and chest as fire builds into
- sharp, explosive movements
- jumps

DYING EMBERS
- Reach a peak, then gradually die down until no sound or movement left
- Stillness
- Small breeze blows ashes away, rolling very gently into a new space

---

DANCE STRUCTURE

AUTUMN = INDIVIDUAL LEAF SEQUENCES (IN CANON) > TRAVEL TO BONFIRE > FIRE BUILDING UP > LEAPING FLAMES > DYING EMBERS > BLOW AWAY

Winter

ICE SHAPES
Using the idea of ice for jagged shapes.

Task 4
- Rise slowly from floor to form three jagged shapes individually
- 'Melt' from one shape to reform into next
- Use tension through body, angles at joints, e.g. elbows Hold each shape for three seconds before melting into next

Task 5
In groups of five.
TRAVEL TO GROUP
- using stiff, angular body shapes, e.g. toes turned in, right elbow bent and lifted
- feet apart, knees bent, right arm bent, palm high, left arm bent, palm low

Perhaps keep repeating a pattern of three or four movements.

SNOWFLAKES
Build three group shapes – snowflake structure
- use each other to build on, over, under
- along floor and into air

DANCE STRUCTURE

WINTER = INDIVIDUAL ICE SHAPES > TRAVEL TO GROUP> SNOWFLAKES

When both Autumn and Winter sections are complete you could join them together

---

DANCE STRUCTURE

INDIVIDUAL LEAF SEQUENCES (CANON) > TRAVEL TO BONFIRE >FIRE BUILDING
UP > LEAPING FLAMES > DYING EMBERS > BLOW AWAY > INDIVIDUAL ICE
SHAPES > TRAVEL TO GROUP > SNOWFLAKES

Learning outcomes

PERFORMANCE perform specific skills and movement patterns with accuracy

COMPOSITION explore, improvise and choose appropriate material to create new motifs
from a given stimulus
compose, develop and adapt motifs to make dance phrases and use
these in longer dances
APPRECIATION talk about the relationship between dance and its accompaniment
suggest ways to develop technique and composition

HEALTH AND SAFETY
- Are the children wearing footwear and clothing that are safe and help their learning?
- Is the space safe and clear enough to work in?
- Are the children aware of others in the class when they are moving around?
- Have all the children warmed up and cooled down properly?

Expectations

When carrying out the type of activities and tasks in this unit

Most children will be able to: compose motifs and plan dances creatively and collaboratively in groups; adapt and refine the way they use weight, space and rhythm in their dances to express themselves in the movement they use; show an understanding of safe exercising; recognise and comment on dances, showing an understanding of interpretation; suggest ways to improve their own and other people's work.

Some children will not have made so much progress. They will be able to: create and perform simple dances; take part in group dances; take part in discussion about the structure of the dance or final performance; show some understanding of how to exercise carefully in dance; use simple words to talk about their own and other people's work.

Some children will have progressed further. They will be able to: plan and perform dances confidently; use their understanding of composition to create dance phrases for themselves and others in their group; show expression in their dances and sensitivity to accompaniment; show understanding of the benefits of warming up for a dance performance; identify the form and structure of a dance; make imaginative suggestions on how to improve their own and other people's work.

Key Stage 2 - Key Stage 3

5. Using a film theme

e.g. Austin Powers
(4 hours)

In this unit pupils continue to abstract movement from a given stimulus and focus on popular dance styles of the 1960s – related to the *Austin Powers* films. Any well-known film can work equally well, such as the *Harry Potter* series or *The Lion King* and may allow you to access dance styles from different eras and locations around the world. Computer games could also be a starting point. Pupils will explore a range of step and gesture patterns, body shapes and contact work. They will use movement to create humour. They will learn more about dance style and music.

Resources

*   tape/ CD player
*   video of chosen film

Where the unit fits in

This builds on work in earlier units to link movement to make longer phrases of movement. Interpretation of a theme is now a focus. Pupils will develop their skills in working with a partner and a group, and will develop a range of compositional ideas and principles.

Prior Learning

It is helpful if pupils have
*   seen or experienced dances from other times and places
*   composed dances on their own and as part of a group
*   experienced pair or group activities

Learning Objectives

- To select, combine and perform a range of movement patterns influenced by dance styles and music from a different era/culture
- To perform dances showing understanding of style, artistic intention and accompaniment
- To focus on clarity of movement and spatial and group awareness
- To evaluate their own strengths and weaknesses in a performance
- To suggest areas for improvement

Action words

- Depending on the ability of the class this first activity can be teacher led one word at a time or set as a whole task.
- Begin by building up an action word sequence based on:

WALK   JUMP   ROLL   SHAKE   POINT   WALK   SPIN

- Write the words on the white/blackboard to help them remember the order
- Individually each pupil should try out two or three different ideas for each action word and then pick the one they like best
- Encourage them to change levels and directions in some of the actions
- When they have their sequence, get the whole class to perform it to music using eight counts for each action

Performance task

- Doing each action for eight counts is quite easy/ comfortable.
- Let's now cut that in half and
  - perform each on four counts
  - perform each on two counts

Discuss what happens to the movement to make it fit the beats.
e.g.   make it smaller, make it stronger and faster, have less change of direction

DUET
Make a duet using this action word sequence with three rules (write them on the board)
- There must be at least one change of speed.
- There must be at least one change of level
- Both dancers must not always face the same way

The duet will probably be more interesting if every action is not performed for the same length of time.

Challenge task
- Your duet could be very interesting if both dancers are not always performing the same action at the same time, e.g. A is walking as B is shaking
- Lengthen your duet by adding three more action words of your own

Observation task
Watch another pair's duet. Can you identify?
- a change of speed
- a change of level
- the most interesting moment. Why do you think that?
- make one suggestion for improvement to their duet

Give feedback time and change over to let them watch the other duet and give feedback.

AUSTIN POWERS
On the white/blackboard or large sheet of sugar paper draw class together and brainstorm what is known about the film.
e.g. characters, plots, locations, era, costume, music.

Write important names and catchphrases on the board.
Write any other words that are relevant to the film and might suggest action
e.g. spying, running, chasing, flying, explode, secret agent, villain, frozen.

Write any words on the board that describe the kind of film it is.
e.g. funny, slap-stick, sexy, action packed, musical, 1960s.

DUETS
You are going to keep the action sequence that you have made up with your partner, but I want you to *develop* it now so that it fits with our theme of *Austin Powers*. Go back to your duet and pick four words written on the board that give you ideas for how to perform your movements. You may wish to alter them a lot or only a very little.

Examples
- spying
  A does walk and jump with B hiding behind arm and peering round, both roll together B following A
- explode
  Shaking action could start small and get bigger to finally 'explode' making both dancers jump away from each other
- 1960s
  Arm actions from 60s social dance added to the walking i.e. swim arms, thumb over shoulder

Students may pick up on the humour in the film and try to create some humour in their duets. Remind them how important facial expressions are, and also still positions such as Dr. Evil's little finger to his chin.

While they are working on this introduce the film's theme music if you have it. In this case *Soul Bossa Nova* by Quincy Jones. The sound of the music will set an atmosphere or mood for the movement without you having to say too much about it. Those pupils who are able to will use counts, others will just have it as background atmosphere. Both are fine.

Group work

- Join with another pair to make a group of four
- Watch each others' duets then pick out one or two bits from each to teach each other so that the whole group can perform them. Pick ideas that
- would look good with all four dancers in unison or canon
- could be extended/ developed to use the extra two people
- would look good performed by one pair and then the other

Make these into a group dance by including the following:
- the parts selected from the two duets
- adding in two still pictures (images from the film) anywhere in the dance
- repeating a movement motif/idea on a different level or at a different speed
- adding in a definite still starting position and finishing position

Encourage pupils to jump about to different parts of the film as source ideas rather than simply trying to tell its story from start to finish. This should help to avoid miming.

Challenge task
- When your group dance is complete go back and make final improvements making sure you have used a variety of speeds, level and direction
- Can you include one 'surprise' in the movement somewhere in your dance

Observation task
Divide class in half to watch half at a time. Ask each pupil to pick one group to watch. Decide the following things:
- Which is the most successful part of the dance? Why?
- Which is the least successful part of the dance? Why?
- Which is your favourite part using the Austin Powers stimuli? Why?

Use the feedback from this to start a short class discussion on what they think makes a good dance.

CHARACTER NAMES

The idea of this section is to use the letters from a character's name to make either floor or air patterns to trace leading with different parts of the body.

- Start by asking the pupils to think of their initials e.g. KS
- Imagine the first letter is written on the floor. Trace the letter with your right foot.
- What happens if the letter is three times bigger? You may have to stretch, walk etc
- What happens if the letter is three times smaller? Maybe only the toe can make contact with floor, speed up
- What could be going on in the rest of your body? You can lean away, complement the shape with arms etc.
- Encourage the pupils to get as much movement into their bodies as possible. Involve shoulders, head, hips, back – so the movement is as full as possible.

- Imagine the second letter is written on a wall in front of you. Trace it with your elbow, your knee, your nose, your bottom
- What happens if the size changes? (repeat as above)
- What happens if the wall is to the side or behind you? Use body twists and turns

Group work

- Go back to previous groups to make next section
- Choose one character's name from the film
- Make a dance spelling out the name using all members of the group. Use a variety of air and floor patterns.
- You may even be able to make one of the letters using all four bodies. Use actions such as turning, running, rolling and falling to link your letters together

It will be more interesting if you don't all do the same thing at the same time.

Challenge task

You may be able to combine different members of the group doing air and floor patterns for each letter of the name.

When this section is complete, link all three sections together to make a longer dance.

DANCE STRUCTURE:

STARTING POSITIONS > DUETS > GROUPS > CHARACTER NAMES (GROUP)

Learning Outcomes

PERFORMANCE   perform dance step and action patterns in response to a stimulus
show an awareness of rhythm and phrasing of accompaniment
perform movement patterns effectively with a partner

COMPOSITION   create motifs that show a dance idea
choose and develop material to create dances
describe the patterns and forms in a specific dance style

APPRECIATION   use appropriate language to describe, interpret and evaluate their own
and others' work
describe the basic characteristics of a dance style and show
understanding of its social and historical context
suggest ideas to improve performance and composition

HEALTH AND SAFETY
* Are the children wearing footwear and clothing that are safe and help their learning?
* Is the space safe and clear enough to work in?
* Are the children aware of others in the class when they are moving around?
* Have all the children warmed up and cooled down properly?

Expectations

After carrying out the activities in this unit

Most pupils will: remember, refine and repeat short dances with a growing sense of style and artistic intention; show awareness of musical structure, rhythm, mood and phrasing; choose and develop dance material; identify strengths and weaknesses in their own and others' work; suggest ways to improve their performance; talk about dance using appropriate vocabulary; carry out suggestions about how to develop their work.

Some pupils will not have made so much progress. They will: dance with some rhythm and control; show some awareness of style and music; display some understanding of how to recognise and describe simple compositional features and performance skills; develop their dance and skills, with guidance.

Some pupils will have progressed further. They will: develop material imaginatively and with clear understanding of content; show a clear sense of dance style and respond to the music when performing; describe, interpret and evaluate dance with an understanding of style, context and what the dance was intended to communicate; take their own decisions about how to develop their work.

Key Stage Three

6. Time

(4 hours)

In this unit pupils focus specifically on developing their knowledge and understanding of composition. They are encouraged to create dance movements and longer phrases from a variety of visual stimuli related to the subject of time. This process is called abstraction. They will develop their understanding of communicating the choreographic intention as performers and choreographers. They will also develop their understanding of rhythm and using the beat or pulse of their accompaniment.

Resources

*   tape/ CD player
*   photographs, images, drawings of different methods of time telling (some provided)

Where the unit fits in

This builds on work in earlier units to link movement to make longer phrases of movement. Interpretation of a visual stimulus is now a focus. Pupils will be extending their range of skills and increasing their understanding of composition.

Prior Learning

It is helpful if pupils have

*   developed movement motifs in a variety of ways
*   understood and used basic compositional principles
*   experienced pair or group activities

Learning Objectives

*   To improve the consistency, quality and use of their skills
*   To create, develop and structure solo and group motifs
*   To perform dances communicating artistic intention
*   To focus on clarity of movement and spatial and group awareness
*   To describe, analyse, interpret and evaluate choreographic form

Time

Introductory activity

*   Walking medium/slow/fast/aimlessly/with purpose/nervously/triumphantly
*   Imagine you are late for an appointment.
*   How do you travel there? (Quickly)
*   What kind of things do you do? (Look at watch)

Discuss 'Time'

- What is it? What does it mean to you?
- Sometimes it passes very quickly e.g. at a party, enjoying yourself
- Other times very slowly e.g. Maths lessons, day before Christmas
- Ask for other examples

Time is actually very constant.

Rhythm

Try to keep a constant 'tick tock' rhythm

- clapping
- walking

Group work

In threes
- Make a simple group shape with each person on a different level and facing a different direction
- Make a constant 'tick tock' rhythm using, stamping, body percussion and voice. Keep it going
- Using the same rhythm, can you do more than one action each?
- Can you make contact with a partner? (suggest image of a clockwork machine)

Developed rhythm

- Now make a more complex rhythm
- It may consist of voice sounds, claps etc. as well as foot rhythms
- Practise it so that the whole group can repeat it easily

Challenge task

- Can you now take your group's rhythm into a travelling motif - try to use different shapes and directions
- The movements must still fit the rhythm exactly
- The step pattern must be repeatable

The floor pattern may change – backwards, forwards, sideways but the rhythm must be kept at ALL times.

Rhythm sequence

Teach the whole class the Sequence – using specific counts
All begin in space anywhere in room

1 -7	Seven walks anywhere
8	Feet together
9 - 10	Turn head to right then left
11- 12	Return head to look forward
1-12	Repeat three times

Performance task
* We are going to do this sequence to a piece of music with a very steady rhythm. Can you make sure you move each action exactly on the beat?

Observation task
* Join in pairs and watch partner perform the sequence
* Count the sequence as they do it
* Are they keeping in time?
* Is each movement exactly on the beat?
* How could they improve?

Give pupils feedback time then repeat the task with the other partner watching.

Split class into As and Bs (groups from earlier sequence must be in the same half)

DANCE STRUCTURE

RHYTHM SEQUENCE Bs (A STAND STILL) > RHYTHM SEQUENCE As (B STAND STILL) > ALL STAND STILL FOR 8 COUNTS (As FACING RIGHT, Bs FACING LEFT) > Bs MARCH 'OFF STAGE' & As MARCH TO STARTING POSITIONS FOR GROUP RHTHM MOTIF > RHYTHM MOTIF > MARCH OFF & Bs MARCH ON > RHYTHM MOTIF

Telling the time

Set off this activity by setting a homework task to find or draw pictures of different ways of telling the time.

Display the pictures. Make a collage or put each idea on a card to give to one group later.

Discuss various different methods of telling the time:
* Sun   – sundial
* Sand – egg timer
* Wax   – candle

- Water bottle – clock
- Sea – waves/tide
- Machine – clock/watch

- How do they work?
- What ideas do they give us for dance?

Go through each method with the whole class exploring movement ideas for each. Pick out good examples and ask the whole class to copy them.

Sundial
Roundness of the sun
Lines of the rays
Shadow of the sun creeping round the clock
Rise and fall of the sun
Shadows when the sun is obscured – symmetry, asymmetry

Egg Timer
Trickle of sand falling
Shape of hour glass
Movement of mass from one place to another
Accumulation of sand (in heap/pyramid)

Candle
Shape of candle/flame
Speed of wax dripping down side – slows down as solidifies
Racing of two different drips of wax down the side
Disappearing of lines on candle

Water Bottle
Drip of water
Splash of drip hitting water
Ripples from the splash – circles

Tide
Shape of waves
Curling and crashing of waves
Shape of pebbles on the beach
Advancing and retreating of tide/waves
Racing of waves – sea horse

Group work

As a group of three to five
Choose just *one* way of telling the time

Using images from that time source, develop a short dance that includes the whole group.
They may start by using movements they already tried individually.
Could the same movement be performed in unison / canon/ mirrored/ matched as a basis?
One image can be used two or three times to make different movements.
Encourage pupils to develop these ideas by using all the group members to make one picture
Encourage contact between pupils

Example: The Egg Timer

- Start with the whole group making the basic shape of an egg timer lying on the floor
- Two stand and turn on spot with arms making shape of the top half
- Three stand and make still picture of the bottom half with their legs
- All turn/ spin to make tight group shape – the sand granules sitting in the top glass
- One by one all move to a new space using the same step pattern – sand falling
- Repeat the group shape in the new space – the sand granules sitting in the bottom glass

Generally they will use the shape of their chosen method of time telling as their starting point, and from this they can develop other movements based on how it works.

Observation task
Join two groups together to watch each other.
Can you identify two images from their source?
How have they developed them?
Which parts work the best? Why?
Can you suggest one improvement?

Class dance

Organise the groups in your space. Make sure they have a still starting and finishing position.
They each perform their group dances one by one in canon.

Learning Outcomes

PERFORMANCE improvise and perform a range of actions with clarity and control
communicate the idea of their dance and show an increasing sensitivity to the accompaniment and other performers

COMPOSITION create and perform dances taking account of the range of movements they could use, the use and variation of motifs, group relationships and the space available

APPRECIATION   use appropriate terminology to describe, analyse, interpret and evaluate
                dances identify and discuss aspects of composition

HEALTH AND SAFETY
*   Are the children wearing footwear and clothing that are safe and help their learning?
*   Is the space safe and clear enough to work in?
*   Are the children aware of others in the class when they are moving around?
*   Have all the children warmed up and cooled down properly?

Expectations
After carrying out the activities in this unit

Most pupils will perform using a good range of skills and techniques clearly and with expression; develop dance ideas and motifs using pictures as a starting point, develop and adapt their ideas to make longer dances using basic compositional principles; structure their dances effectively; identify qualities in movement; suggest ways of improving quality in their own and others' dances.

Some pupils will not have made so much progress. They will perform some of the basic skills with control and some expression; repeat and adapt basic motifs and ideas with help; use some compositional ideas and structures in their dances; describe the basic structure and intention of their dance; with help, recognise and describe some of the qualities of a dance; carry out compositional work to improve their own dances.

Some pupils will have progressed further. They will perform with expression, fluency and accuracy; devise and develop dance ideas and motifs with a clear view of what they wish to communicate; combine a range of ideas into their dances showing a good understanding of principles of composition; describe dances accurately using dance terminology; identify strengths and weaknesses in their own and others' dances; take the initiative to develop and improve their dances.

7. Colour and Shape

(4 hours)

This unit was originally written based on the Kandinsky painting 'Contact', 1924. The same principles can be applied to using any abstract art work. A template is provided in the unit (page opposite) for pupils to colour as they wish, or you could set a homework task to design an abstract picture using triangles, circles, straight and curvy lines and a brick wall. In this unit pupils develop their knowledge of abstract choreography using a picture or painting as a stimulus. They develop their understanding of communicating mood and emotion through movement.

Resources
- abstract picture or painting
- tape/CD player
- black/whiteboard
- tv and video
- sugar paper and pens

Where the unit fits in
This unit builds on the pupils' ability to use choreographic devices to interpret an abstract idea. This increases their knowledge of dance as an art form and leads well into looking at abstract professional works, different types of dance and the demands of different types of dance technique.

Prior Learning
It is helpful if pupils have:
- knowledge and experience of a range of compositional principles
- used professional dance works on video as a learning resource
- experienced different styles and types of dance

Learning Objectives
- to perform with technical competence and an understanding of dynamics
- to improvise and extend movement ideas on their own and with others
- to use a range of compositional devices
- to communicate the dance idea
- to analyse, interpret and evaluate dances with an understanding of style, context and intention and use this understanding to improve their performance
- to take responsibility for making decisions about how to develop and improve their own and others' work

Colour

Colour enriches our world and a world of black and white is unimaginable. Colours affect our emotions and reflect them, they can make things warm or cold, exciting or peaceful.

Shapes are found naturally in the landscape, sky and sea. They are also made by man, architecture, paintings and sculpture. A mixture of symmetrical and assymetrical shapes make our world balanced and interesting.

Task 1

- Ask pupils, in groups of four, to list as many colours as they can think of (on sugar paper – quite large)
  Next to each colour get them to write associated emotions, such as

  RED =   Danger   Anger   Dynamic

  BLACK = Sad   Powerful   Mourning

- Teach a very simple phrase using the words

  Turn   Curl   Jump   Slide   Balance

Remember action words may apply to the whole body or just one body part

- Pick two of the colours from their sheet
- First, dance the phrase with the qualities of one colour, then again with the qualities of the second colour

Observation task
- Watch a partner perform both phrases
- How do they differ?
- Try to use very descriptive language. This will give you useful language for talking about dynamics

Task 2

- In pairs think of three symmetric and three asymmetric shapes (refer to nature and famous buildings). Remind pupils of different levels, spacing

- Add the 'best' symmetric and asymmetric shapes to the phrase
Turn   Curl   Jump   Slide   Balance **(danced in one colour only)**

e.g. TURN > SLIDE > SYMMETRICAL SHAPE > CURL > ASSYMMETRICAL SHAPE >BALANCE

Emphasise the importance of holding the shapes still for a count of three to add emphasis to the shapes.

Task 3

- Look at your abstract picture/painting
- Discuss its composition, colour and shape

What ideas can the shapes and colours give us?

> e.g. straight lines = sharp, angles, pointing somewhere.
>   soft rounded lines = circling round something/someone.

How can we use shape?
- copy as floor patterns
- copy as air patterns
- make the shape with one body or groups of bodies
- give us directions to face

Individual task

- Choose a shape from the painting
  Use that shape to make a small phrase which must include travel, fall, stretch

- Remind the class of work on the emotions of different colours

  Play around with some of the movements in your phrase to see how you might
  perform them differently if they were different colours
  How will the quality/dynamics change?
  Will the size of the movements alter?
  Will the level or speed change?

Performance task

Pick two colours from the painting and perform your phrase accordingly.

e.g.   Yellow version = bright, lifted, large and open.

Red version = strong, angry, dangerous/risky

Group work

(three to five pupils)

Teacher allocates or group chooses a *section* of the painting to work from, such as

- blue circle
- yellow triangle
- black parallel lines
- brick wall

Laminating will preserve pictures for use with many groups.

Viewfinders used in the Art department are excellent to focus on one area.

The group should discuss how they might interpret their section of the painting using information gathered about movement formation and development, colour and shape.

e.g. blue circle, think of:

- shape – circular pathways, rounded movements
- whether the shape is solid or hollow
- what mood does blue evoke

Task 4

Using their individual shape and colour ideas, their Task 2 phrases and any new ideas from the painting, create a short dance based on their section of the painting.

Dance structure

By now the pupils should be able to devise a structure of their own rather than relying on something set by the teacher. Encourage them to find a creative response to organising their movement. Remember there are really no rights or wrongs – so have fun with it.

Suggestion

Use the painting section as a map

Decide on a 'route' through the painting (they could draw it with felt pen on clear acetate paper laid over the top) and structure the dance using each shape and colour met on that route.

Suggestion
Each person in the group represents a certain shape
Use the different sizes and colours of the shapes in the painting to structure each individual part.
What could happen where different shapes meet?
* cross collide lift join
* mirror unison canon

An aim of the project could be to make a painting that moves. The teacher would need to direct the joining of the various small sections to make a whole class dance.

Observation task
* Watch one group perform their dance
* What shapes and colours do you think they have based their dance on? Why?
* Which is the most successful part of the dance? Why?
* What one suggestion do you have to improve their dance?

Learning Outcomes

PERFORMANCE: improvise and perform a range of actions with technical competence, clarity of shape and dynamics, and showing sensitivity to phrasing and rhythm
communicate the idea of their dance and show an increasing sensitivity to the accompaniment and other performers

COMPOSITION: create and perform dances taking account of the range of movements they could use,
the use and variation of motifs, group relationships and the space available demonstrate an understanding of different choreographic principles and use them with increasing competence

APPRECIATION: use appropriate terminology to describe, analyse, interpret and evaluate dances
identify and discuss aspects of composition showing evidence of artistic, aesthetic and cultural understanding

HEALTH AND SAFETY
* Are the children wearing footwear and clothing that are safe and help their learning?
* Is the space safe and clear enough to work in?
* Are the children aware of others in the class when they are moving around?
* Have all the children warmed up and cooled down properly?

Expectations

After carrying out the activities in this unit

Most pupils will perform using a good range of skills and techniques clearly and with expression; develop dance ideas and motifs using pictures as a starting point, develop and adapt their ideas to make longer dances using a variety of compositional principles; structure their dances effectively; identify qualities in movement; reflect upon their own work and that of their peers; make decisions that improve the quality of their own and others' dances.

Some pupils will not have made so much progress. They will perform some of the basic skills with control and some expression; repeat and adapt basic motifs and ideas with help; use some simple choreographic principles in their dances; describe the basic structure and intention of their dance; with help, recognise and describe some of the qualities of a dance; present some ideas to develop and improve dances.

Some pupils will have progressed further. They will perform with very good technical and expressive skills; devise and develop dance ideas and motifs with a clear view of what they wish to communicate; combine a range of ideas into their dances showing sophisticated understanding of principles of composition; describe dances accurately using dance terminology; identify strengths and weaknesses in their own and others' dances; take the initiative to develop and improve their dances.

8. Our World

(4 hours)

This unit explores developing dance movements from every day life and movement. This is called abstraction. The focus of the unit is developing pupils knowledge and understanding of composition. They develop their understanding of communicating the choreographic intention as performers and choreographers. The themes of this unit lend themselves well to a cross- curricular project. The environment is a comprehensive subject that lends itself very well to dance. Suggested here is one idea based on the theme of cruelty to animals; those hunted for their fur. One other related activity could be mask-making (hunting scene).

Resources
- tape/ CD player
- photos from fashion magazines
- literature from animal rights groups
- markers to indicate catwalk

Where the unit fits in
This builds on work in earlier units to links movement to make longer phrases of movement. Interpretation of a theme, visual stimulus and text is now a focus. Pupils will be extending their range of skills and increasing their understanding of composition.

Prior Learning
It is helpful if pupils have
- developed movement motifs in a variety of ways
- understood and used basic compositional principles
- experienced pair or group activities

Learning Objectives
- To improve the consistency, quality and use of their skills
- To create, develop and structure solo and group motifs
- To perform dances communicating artistic intention
- To focus on clarity of movement and spatial and group awareness
- To describe, analyse, interpret and evaluate choreographic form

The catwalk

'Vanity, cruelty, murder' – an investigation into the fur trade.

It would be useful to gather as much resource material on the subject as possible, prior to starting the project. Selected information and facts could be used in the performance.
- The characters we will use in this unit are models, photographers and demonstrators
- Discuss characteristics/ personalities of each. How do they move? Facial expressions?
- Try out some movement ideas for each. Remember you are trying to find fuller dance ideas, not just mime the story.

Models

Show class magazines/videos of fashion models to give them some ideas on how to 'pose' (you will probably find that children will find this easy)
Copy some of the poses from the magazines. Experiment with walking as a model down an imaginary catwalk. Stop three or four times to make a pose. Face a different direction each time. Can you change levels? Show off the clothes – accentuate different parts of your body to show the clothing item e.g shoes, gloves, jacket, hat

Performance task
- Can you walk and pose with the confidence of a model? Hips leading, wide shoulders, chin lifted.

Photographers

Find three or four different positions a photographer may get into e.g. kneeling/crouching to get the best shot, calling to model to look his/her way, calling over shoulder to assistant, loading new film. Add in simple action words between these positions to make a repeatable sequence.

e.g turn > taking photo > slide > calling to model > jump > call assistant > balance > load film

Challenge task
Give your sequence a rhythm by performing each movement to four counts.

Anti-Fur Demonstrators

Find two or three positions a demonstrator may get into e.g. holding up banners, shouting anti-fur slogans, lying down to obstruct the show, linking arms with fellow protestors to make a barrier.
Add in different action words between these positions to make a repeatable sequence.

e.g. stamp > banners > spin > shouting slogan > fall > obstruction > spiral up > link arms

Group work

Divide the class into groups of six
Each group will need:
2 models
1 photographer
2 Anti-fur demonstrators

The group should mark out an imaginary catwalk.

Using the ideas you have just worked on, the two models move down the catwalk and back with the photographer at the side. The two anti -fur demonstrators wait slightly away from the catwalk. Play a piece of funky music to create atmosphere. Some pupils may be happy to provide this.

Example
Models: Walk for four counts. Pose for four counts. Repeat this eight times
(The models are supposed to be wearing fur coats or leather products)

Photographer: Needs four poses that should compliment those of the models.
Aim for strong body positions on different levels

Anti-Fur Demonstrators: Repeat their pattern of movements on four counts each.
When models and photographers reach end of catwalk, the demonstrators shout 'STOP

This is a cue for the music to be turned off and the models and photographers should freeze.

The demonstrators verbally deliver their accusations to the models/photographers (using information from research). They will need to end with a strong statement such as 'Once the animals roamed free before they were hunted by man'.

Hunting scene

Teach a basic phrase to the whole class based on an animal being hunted. This will be developed later in pair work. You could use these words:

Strike   **Chase**   **Hide**   **Jump**   **Fall**

In pairs
- One person will represent the animal (mask)
- One person will represent the hunter

Animals
Hunters

• Hunters stalk animals – moving in on them

Each pair will create a short dance to depict the struggle between the man and the animal. Remind them of the phrase you taught. How could they develop the actions? Encourage them to move away from simple mime by using repetition, changing speed, level and direction of movement, unison and canon.

Observation task
Watch another pair's dance.
Can you see two developments of the earlier taught phrase? What are they?
Make one suggestion to improve their use of space.

• Man overpowers animals.
Either teach a set study or create one with the pupils based on the image of growing/reaching upwards. Everyone learns the study. Use ideas of creating shapes with alternating body parts reaching upwards for survival. Use standing shapes and floor work. Link with turns, pauses and rolls to fall/drop before reaching up again.

DUET
Think of the study as one half of a duet – representing the animals working to survive. With only the 'animal' role dancing the set study, choreograph the other person's role as 'man.' to make a duet.

- Find movements for 'man' to cause the destruction of 'animal' i.e. think of action/re-action what could 'man' do to cause the 'animal's' downward movements from the study – push downwards with elbow, lean against 'animal' with back, closing in the space around the 'animal'
- Encourage pupils to use a variety of body parts to lead the movement, not just arms
- Use any images of natural resources being used up or destroyed
  e.g. trees felled, seals clubbed, animals trapped for fur

Observation task
- Watch another pair's duet
- Identify three different body parts that lead attacking or defending movements
- Are they using their arms too much? If so can you suggest another idea to improve their dance

Performance task
Using the suggestions just given to you, work on improving your duet, particularly moving

smoothly between movements so that the movement flows. Make sure it is a fuller performance than simply miming the fight.

DANCE STRUCTURE:

CATWALK > DEMONSTATORS STOP THE SHOW > DEMONSTATORS DELIVER ACCUSATIONS > MOVE TO SPACE IN PAIRS > HUNTING DUETS

Learning Outcomes

PERFORMANCE improvise and perform a range of actions with clarity and control
communicate the idea of their dance and show an increasing sensitivity to the accompaniment and other performers

COMPOSITION create and perform dances taking account of the range of movements they could use, the use and variation of motifs, group relationships and the space available

APPRECIATION use appropriate terminology to describe, analyse, interpret and evaluate dances
identify and discuss aspects of composition

HEALTH AND SAFETY
- Are the children wearing footwear and clothing that are safe and help their learning?
- Is the space safe and clear enough to work in?
- Are the children aware of others in the class when they are moving around?
- Have all the children warmed up and cooled down properly?

Expectations

After carrying out the activities in this unit

Most pupils will perform using a good range of skills and techniques clearly and with expression; develop dance ideas and motifs using pictures as a starting point, develop and adapt their ideas to make longer dances using basic compositional principles; structure their dances effectively; identify qualities in movement; suggest ways of improving quality in their own and others' dances.

Some pupils will not have made so much progress. They will perform some of the basic skills with control and some expression; repeat and adapt basic motifs and ideas with help; use some compositional ideas and structures in their dances; describe the basic structure and intention of their dance; with help, recognise and describe some of the qualities of a dance; carry out compositional work to improve their own dances.

Some pupils will have progressed further. They will perform with expression, fluency and accuracy; devise and develop dance ideas and motifs with a clear view of what they wish to communicate; combine a range of ideas into their dances showing a good understanding of principles of composition; describe dances accurately using dance terminology; identify strengths and weaknesses in their own and others' dances; take the initiative to develop and improve their dances.

9. Horror!

(4 hours)

In this unit pupils focus specifically on developing their knowledge and understanding of composition. They are encouraged to create dance movements and longer phrases from a theme. This process is called abstraction. A variety of source material could be used to introduce the subject including ghost stories, pictures and videos. They will develop their understanding of communicating the choreographic intention as performers and choreographers.

Resources

- tape/ CD player
- source material e.g. ghost story, picture
- white/ blackboard

Where the unit fits in

This builds on work in earlier units to link movement to make longer phrases of movement. Interpretation of a theme is now a focus. Pupils will be extending their range of skills and increasing their understanding of composition.

Prior Learning

It is helpful if pupils have
- developed movement motifs in a variety of ways
- understood and used basic compositional principles
- experienced pair or group activities

Learning Objectives

- to improve the consistency, quality and use of their skills
- to create, develop and structure solo and group motifs
- to perform dances communicating artistic intention
- to focus on clarity of movement and spatial and group awareness
- to describe, analyse, interpret and evaluate choreographic form

Horror

Begin by brainstorming the subject on the board – ask for any images we associate with horror/ ghost stories, e.g. cobwebs, blood, zombies, witches, ghost trains, murder.
Maybe even tell the class a ghost story!
Try out some of these ideas one at a time with the whole class. If someone comes up with an interesting idea – all copy it.

If the teacher feels confident he/she could begin the unit by teaching the whole class a study based on the horror images. Pupils could then use the whole study or movements from it to develop their basic dance structure. However this is not necessary.

Group work

Divide class into groups of four.
Choose three images from all of those on the board. Make *three* still pictures using the whole group.
Encourage interesting use of level, direction and contact between dancers.
Encourage the pictures to be distorted and gruesome!

Graveyard

The group's starting point is to create a still graveyard scene – bodies, tombstones, grave diggers, trees, shadows.
- Hold the image completely still
- Gradually start to move your bodies – only very slight at first then gradually increasing the size of the movement. (The image here is of the wind moving trees, shadows

moving, animals creeping) Use your eyes to look around you – build up the tension
- Add a sudden movement – to frighten / alarm audience
- What happens next? Find a conclusion to this scene
- suggestions – corpse rises out of grave
- the whole scene settles back down to stillness after the sudden movement
- gravediggers are attacked by the trees

Observation task
- Watch another group perform their graveyard dance
- How have they been successful in creating a sense of tension/ horror?
- Can you give suggestions to make two movements more frightening or uncomfortable to watch. Think about the angle of heads and joints and facial expression
- Feedback to the group and then they do the same for you

Tumbleweed
Use the idea of tumbleweed rolling slowly down a deserted road
Use very slow rolling/ rotation to move out of the graveyard scene

Performance task
This movement needs a ghostly quality. Can you make it very slow, smooth and sustained?
Do you have to be on your feet? Do you have to be travelling forwards?

Ghost Train
Use group to make a moving ghost train.
Encourage pupils to face different directions, lean on each other, use distorted body shape, limping, carrying.
Make a complex group shape and find a way to slowly move forwards to another space
As well as the main body of the train they might also have train wheels, man walking ahead of the train with flag, dead bodies on the train etc.

Murder
Choose a particularly gruesome murder idea
Act it out first. Dance is not real life – take reality as a starting point and abstract away from it. This means making the movement much fuller by using repetition, level, speed and size change and adding in more actions.

Make a short sequence based on your murder idea:
- Enlarge/ exaggerate three movements

- Add in a turn, pause and slide
- Repeat one movement three times
- Do one movement in canon
- Give the sequence counts and make as rhythmic as possible

Observation task
- Watch another group perform their murder dance
- Are they just miming of have they developed the movement to make it much fuller?
- Which part works the best? Why?
- Make one suggestion to improve their dance
- Swap over so they do the same for you

Take a few minutes to improve your dance following the feedback you have had.

The final step is to link all the various sections together to make one long dance.

DANCE STRUCTURE

GRAVEYARD > TUMBLEWEED > PICTURE 1 > GHOST TRAIN > PICTURE 2 > MURDER > PICTURE 3.

Learning Outcomes

PERFORMANCE   improvise and perform a range of actions with clarity and control
communicate the idea of their dance and show an increasing sensitivity to the accompaniment and other performers

COMPOSITION   create and perform dances taking account of the range of movements they could use, the use and variation of motifs, group relationships and the space available

APPRECIATION   use appropriate terminology to describe, analyse, interpret and evaluate dances
identify and discuss aspects of composition

HEALTH AND SAFETY
- Are the children wearing footwear and clothing that are safe and help their learning?
- Is the space safe and clear enough to work in?
- Are the children aware of others in the class when they are moving around?
- Have all the children warmed up and cooled down properly?

Expectations

After carrying out the activities in this unit

Most pupils will perform using a good range of skills and techniques clearly and with expression; develop dance ideas and motifs using horror themes as a starting point, develop and adapt their ideas to make longer dances using basic compositional principles; structure their dances effectively; identify qualities in movement; suggest ways of improving quality in their own and others' dances.

Some pupils will not have made so much progress. They will perform some of the basic skills with control and some expression; repeat and adapt basic motifs and ideas with help; use some compositional ideas and structures in their dances; describe the basic structure and intention of their dance; with help, recognise and describe some of the qualities of a dance; carry out compositional work to improve their own dances.

Some pupils will have progressed further. They will perform with expression, fluency and accuracy; devise and develop dance ideas and motifs with a clear view of what they wish to communicate; combine a range of ideas into their dances showing a good understanding of principles of composition; describe dances accurately using dance terminology; identify strengths and weaknesses in their own and others' dances; take the initiative to develop and improve their dances.

How to use the glossaries

This glossary was originally written for secondary school students by Heather Worrall, a colleague of mine. It is an excellent resource and, with her permission, I have adapted it as a suggested aid for your teaching and also for any further reading you may do about dance.

The glossary was originally intended to encourage the learning of vocabulary for dance, step by step, through observing examples from professional works as well as through doing. It was not intended to be a text book or to be used to encourage static lessons involving the memorizing of words. Pupils should be as practically engaged with dance as possible and the glossary was designed with this in mind. I have kept a small core of suggested masterworks for those of you who have access to professional dance videos/DVDs.

Each word carries with it a broad definition and most words carry a resource suggestion. These suggestions detail snippets of masterworks that may be shown to exemplify the word in question. The masterworks are merely examples which back up the word being introduced and which offer examples of good practice that pupils might strive towards. I have always found showing pupils examples of professional works very helpful in my teaching. They can be an inspiration in many ways.

I have chosen masterworks from DVDs/videos available from Dance Books Ltd (see *Resources Finder* page137). They are what is known as mainstream contemporary dance.

There are two versions of the glossary – both reference Mathew Bourne's *Swan Lake* as I have used this successfully with all age groups over and over again. Then each glossary references examples from other DVDs. Which one you choose will be down to personal preference. Most of the vocabulary examples can be found in these works. There are a few words which cannot, and I have given other masterworks as reference.

Example

A teacher wishing to teach 'contact' to Year 5 may teach a small phrase including contact between two or more dancers. This may or may not be based on a masterwork. S/he may explain what points of contact may be used, write examples on the board, give teaching points for safe and correct execution and show an example of its use in a masterwork. Pupils are then learning the word at a deep level and are more likely to remember it. The inclusion of 'contact' in this glossary would be as follows:

Contact	Two or more dancers physically manipulating each other. Bearing, lifting and supporting weight.	• *Episodes*: throughout • *Act 2 Swan Lake* – swan/prince duets

GLOSSARY ONE

Suggested resources:
For Bird With Love, Alvin Ailey
Witness, Alvin Ailey
Episodes, Ulysses Dove
Swan Lake, Mathew Bourne

Vocabulary	Definition	Resource
Abstraction	Either making a movement larger than life, or reducing it to its smallest and most minimal state. Useful for gestural movement.	• *Swan Lake* Act 1 –– dressing the prince
Appreciation	Evaluating and describing dance.	
Ballet	A genre that originated in Italy, became popular in 18ᵗʰ century France and highly skilled in 19ᵗʰ century Russia. A codified classical technique originally intended to impress the monarchy.	• *Swan Lake* • *Sleeping Beauty* • *Nutcracker*
Bound	Movement that has a definite finishing point, although this does not have to be the ending of the dance.	• Section 1 *For Bird With Love* • *Episodes*: throughout
Canon	Dancing one after the other, creating an overlap or ripple effect. Usually done using the same movement for each dancer.	• Act 2 *Swan Lake* – swans on lake • *Episodes*: throughout

Centre	The region of and around the abdominal muscles.	• Act 2 *Swan Lake* – clear on male swans
Centred	Controlling the centre with a feeling of the body weight dropping through the body into the floor.	• Act 2 *Swan Lake* – swans on lake • *Witness*: throughout
Choreographer	The creator of the dance.	
Choreography	The making of the dance. Movement.	
Climax	The singular most exciting highlight of the dance which all movement is building towards. The peak of the dance.	• Seen in all masterworks
Composition	Creating or choreographing a dance.	
Contact	Two or more dancers physically manipulating each other. Bearing, lifting and supporting weight.	• *Episodes*: throughout • *Act 2 Swan Lake* – swan/prince duets
Contact Improvisation	Making up movement on the spot with a partner, by physically manipulating each other. A frequent starting point for much New Dance & Physical Theatre.	• See work of DV8
Contemporary Dance	A genre that was pioneered by Martha Graham in 1920s America as a rebellion against ballet. Many techniques now used within the genre, many of the influenced by Graham.	• All four masterwork examples
Contraction	A pull in of the abdominals with curve in the lower back, breathing out. Graham-based.	• *Witness:* throughout

Copy & Contrast	Either copying a partner's movement/essence of movement, or contrasting the movement in terms of level, dynamic, shape etc.	• Act 2 *Swan Lake* – swans on lake
Counts	The process by which dancers establish the rhythm of the dance, by counting the bars and phrasing. Frequently, but not always, used in conjunction with music.	• Very clear in 1st section *From Bird with Love*
Cunningham	Merce Cunningham, American dancer/choreographer. Trained with Graham but formed own company to explore formalist work. Formed own technique now used widely.	• *Changing Steps* (Cunningham,1989)
Devices	e.g. canon, repetition, motif development. The methodologies of choreography.	• Most masterworks will show a variety of devices
Direct correlation	Movement that follows the musical score exactly or very closely. Rhythm, tempo, structure and mood may be mirrored.	• Section 1 *From Bird with Love* • Act 1 *Swan Lake* – nightclub scene • Also much classical ballet
Downstage	The area towards the front of the stage.	
Duet	A dance for two people.	• *Episodes*: various • Act 2 *Swan Lake* – prince and swan
Dynamics (time) Dynamics (force & flow)	e.g. fast, sudden, slow speeds. The energy used to execute a movement.	• *From Bird with Love*: contrasting dynamics in various sections

Earthbound	Dancing with the body weight moving into or near the ground. There may be jumps but the emphasis is on the landing rather than on the time spent in the air.	• *Episodes*: throughout
Elevation	Light, jumpy movement which may also involve large leaps.	• *Episodes*: various • Act 2 *Swan Lake* – various by swans on lake
Expressive Dance	Dance that uses the whole body and movement to express an idea, mood, story or emotion.	• *From Bird with Love*: throughout • *Swan Lake:* throughout
Flex	Turning the toes and foot up towards the ceiling.	• *Witness*: throughout
Floor Patterns	The patterns and lines that dancers trace on the floor, through the travelling of their movements.	• Found in all masterworks listed. A good start would be Act 2 *Swan Lake* – swans on lake
Flow	How movements and phrases link together to form a whole dance.	• Section 2 *From Bird with Love* • *Witness*
Fluid	Flowing movements that join together seamlessly.	• Act 2 *Swan Lake* – swans on lake
Focus	Looking with confidence and purpose. Imperative for performance.	• Section 1 *From Bird with Love* • Act 2 *Swan Lake* – lead swan solo
Free	A movement that has no definite finishing point, leading straight into the next movement e.g. a flung arm or swing. Contrasts with 'Bound'.	• *Witness*: various

Genre	A specific style of dance with a codified technique or set of ideals e.g. Ballet, Contemporary, Jazz.	• Act 1 *Swan Lake* – nightclub scene: rock 'n roll influence • *From Bird with Love*: jazz influence
Gesture	A movement with no transfer of weight. Frequently preoccupied with the arms and hands.	• Act 1 *Swan Lake* – opening scene
Graham	American dancer/ choreographer. A pioneer of contemporary dance. In dance terms her influence is equal to Stravinsky and Picasso's in music and art. Own technique now used widely in dancers' training (source: *Dance Handbook*, 1990, p. 67).	• *From Bird with Love* & *Witness:* throughout – influence of Graham technique
Highlight	A moment of particular interest and excitement within a dance.	• Most works will demonstrate highlights
Jazz Dance	A genre that originated in Black America, involving isolations, little use of devices and a degree of sensuality. Widely used in commercial work and musicals.	• Influence seen throughout *From Bird with Love*
Levels	High, medium and low. Effective when used in contrast in duets and group dances.	• Section 1 *From Bird with Love* • Act 2 *Swan Lake* – swans on lake
Linear	Clear and strong lines, usually used to describe positions of the arms, legs and to describe floor patterns.	• *Episodes:* throughout • Act 2 *Swan Lake* – swans on lake
Lyrical	Light, fluid movement. Often slightly elevated.	
Motif	A short phrase or movement that represents the essence of the dance. Usually repeated and/or developed later on.	• Act 2 *Swan Lake:* – swans on lake: wings, head rolls, dipping, beak motifs

Motif Development	The development or a motif, how it changes e.g. slow it down, change the level etc.	• Act 2 *Swan Lake* – swans on lake
Narrative	Movement that tells a story.	•*Swan Lake:* throughout • *From Bird with Love:* various sections
New Dance	'A mini revolution which started (in the 1970s)…partly about choreographic experiment and partly about altering the way people think about dance…open to a wide range of influences and ideas' (Mackrell, J 1992, p1).	• *Strange Fish* (Newson, 1992) • *Flesh & Blood* (Anderson, 1991)
Organic	Where one movement grows out of another.	
Parallel	Feet an inch or so apart, toes facing the front.	
Percussive	Movement (usually footwork) that is rhythmic, bound, earthbound and centred. Frequently making noise with the feet.	•Act 1 *Swan Lake* – nightclub scene • Act 2 *Swan Lake* – comedy swan quartet
Performance	Showing a dance for an audience – the best you can do. Qualities needed include confidence, focus, energy, thinking ahead, visual communication, listening skills.	• Any masterwork will demonstrate the qualities required for performance eg. *Witness*
Phrase	A sequence of movements.	
Plié	A bend of the knees with the feet in place on the floor, forming a diamond shape in between. May be in parallel or turned out with the feet in one of the five positions. A balletic term.	• All ballets show the use of plié as a transitory position. • *Witness*

Projection	Letting the energy flow out of the movement, using a strong focus. Projecting towards a partner and/or audience.	•Section 1 *From Bird with Love* • Act 2 *Swan Lake* – swan/prince duet
Quality	How you dance rather than what you do. Paying attention to detail, sustaining movement, focus and confidence, not cutting corners.	• Any masterwork will demonstrate quality
Quartet	A dance for four people.	• Act 2 *Swan Lake* – comedy swan quartet
Release	A technique within the contemporary dance genre involving relaxing into the movement, releasing body tension, working within the capabilities of the body and using breath control. Now influencing a large amount of work.	• *Strange Fish* (Newson, 1992) • *Wyoming* (Davies, 1989)
Repetition	Repeating movements and phrases either intact or developed.	•*Episodes:* throughout • Act 3 *Swan Lake* – final scene
Simple canon	Dancer A followed by dancer B followed by C, each dancing a complete phrase and ending at different times creating an overlapping effect.	
Social Dance	Dancing for fun, usually involving communities e.g. discos, barn dances, country dances, etc. Also embraces Folk Dance. Both can be used as a basis for Theatre Dance.	Social/Folk Dance as stimulus for Theatre Dance • *From Bird with Love* – jazz • Act 2 *Swan Lake* – nightclub scene: rock n' roll

Solo	A dance for one person.	• Acts 2 & 3 *Swan Lake* – lead swan/ball guest
Spatial awareness	Being aware of your own space, where others are in space, anticipating collisions etc.	
Spotting	The process which stops you falling over when turning. Looking at a spot in front of you until your body is turned 90°, then whipping the head round to look at it again.	• Act 2 *Swan Lake* – lead swan solo
Staccato	Sharp, strong, punctuated, stabbing movement.	• *From Bird with Love* • Act 2 Swan Lake – nightclub scene
Stage left	The area to the left of you as you face the audience.	
Stage right	The area to the right of you as you face the audience.	
Stimulus	The starting point for the dance idea. May be music, a picture, a story, a mood etc.	• *Swan Lake* – story, music • *From Bird with Love* – biography, music • *Witness* – religion • *Episodes* – shape, mood
Sustained	Stretching a movement to its very limit before moving to the next.	• *Witness*
Symmetry	Movements or patterns that are the same on both sides.	• Act 2 *Swan Lake* swans on lake
Technique	Skill. A codified way of doing set exercises in order to build strength, stamina and facility. Codified techniques include Ballet, Graham, Cunningham.	

Tension	Controlled contracted energy held within the body. Various degrees of tension may be used.	
Ternary Form	A dance taking the form of verse, chorus, verse, chorus etc or ABA.	
Theatre Dance	Dances that are made specifically for an audience. Usually, although not always, performed in a theatre.	• All masterworks are examples of Theatre Dance
Tilt	A two-dimensional bend to the side from above the waist. Movement must be centred. Usually accompanied by linear and/or curved arms. Cunningham-based.	• Act 2 *Swan Lake* – swans on lake
Transition	A linking movement or phrase. The link between phrases.	
Trio	A dance for three people.	• *Episodes*
Triplets	3 walks: Down, up, up. Repeated on alternate sides and travelling forwards, backwards, sideways or using a combination. Centred. Graham & Cunningham-based.	
Turnout	Turning the legs out from the hip sockets with the thighs, knees and toes aligned.	• *Witness* : various • *Swan Lake:* throughout
Unison	Dancing altogether at the same time, usually using the same movement for maximum effect.	• Section 1 *From Bird with Love* • Act 2 *Swan Lake* – swans on lake
Upstage	The area towards the back of the stage.	• Used effectively Act 3 *Swan Lake* – ball scene

GLOSSARY TWO

Suggested resources:

Lonely Town, Lonely Street, Robert North
Intimate Pages, Christopher Bruce
Sergeant Early's Dream, Christopher Bruce
Swan Lake, Mathew Bourne

Vocabulary	Definition	Resource
Abstraction	Either making a movement larger than life, or reducing it to its smallest and most minimal state. Useful for gestural movement.	• *Swan Lake* Act 1 – dressing the prince
Appreciation	Evaluating and describing dance.	
Ballet	A genre that originated in Italy, became popular in 18th century France and highly skilled in 19th century Russia. A codified classical technique originally intended to impress the monarchy.	• *Swan Lake* • *Sleeping Beauty* • *Nutcracker*
Bound	Movement that has a definite finishing point, although this does not have to be the ending of the dance.	• Section 1 *Lonely Town, Lonely Street* • Section 9 *Sergeant Early's Dream*
Canon	Dancing one after the other, creating an overlap or ripple effect. Usually done using the same movement for each dancer.	• Act 2 *Swan Lake* – swans on lake • *Intimate Pages* – 1st female duet (in grey dresses)

Centre	The region of and around the abdominal muscles.	• Seen clearly in Act 2 *Swan Lake* – male swans
Centred	Controlling the centre with a feeling of the bodyweight dropping through the body into the floor.	• Act 2 *Swan Lake* – swans • *Sergeant Early's Dream:* throughout
Choreographer	The creator of the dance.	
Choreography	The making of the dance. Movement.	
Climax	The singular most exciting highlight of the dance which all movement is building towards. The peak of the dance.	• Entrance of mystery guest at ball Act 3 *Swan Lake*
Composition	Creating or choreographing a dance.	
Contact	Two or more dancers physically manipulating each other. Bearing, lifting and supporting weight.	• *Intimate Pages:* throughout • *Act 2 Swan Lake* – swan/prince duets
Contact Improvisation	Making up movement on the spot with a partner, by physically manipulating each other. A frequent starting point for much New Dance & Physical Theatre.	• See work of DV8
Contemporary Dance	A genre that was pioneered by Martha Graham in 1920s America as a rebellion against ballet. Many techniques now used within the genre, many of the influenced by Graham.	• All four masterwork examples See various in video excerpts at start of *Three by Rambert*
Contraction	A pull in of the abdominals with curve in the lower back, breathing out. Graham-based.	•*Lonely Town, Lonely Street* throughout

Copy & Contrast	Either copying a partner's movement/essence of movement, or contrasting the movement in terms of level, dynamic, shape etc.	• Act 2 *Swan Lake* – swans on lake • Intimate Pages: throughout • Section 4 *Sergeant Early's Dream*
Counts	The process by which dancers establish the rhythm of the dance, by counting the bars and phrasing. Frequently, but not always, used in conjunction with music.	• Section 1 *Lonely Town, Lonely Street* – walking on the count
Cunningham	Merce Cunningham, American dancer/choreographer. Trained with Graham but formed own company to explore formalist work. Formed own technique now used widely.	• *Changing Steps* (Cunningham,1989) • *Sergeant Early's Dream*: throughout
Devices	e.g. canon, repetition, motif development. The methodologies of choreography.	• Most masterworks will show a variety of devices
Direct correlation	Movement that follows the musical score exactly or very closely. Rhythm, tempo, structure and mood may be mirrored.	• Section 1 *Lonely Town, Lonely Street* • Act 1 *Swan Lake* – nightclub scene • Also much classical ballet
Downstage	The area towards the front of the stage.	
Duet	A dance for two people.	• *Intimate Pages:* throughout • Act 2 *Swan Lake* – prince and swan
Dynamics (time) Dynamics (force & flow)	e.g. fast, sudden, slow speeds. The energy used to execute a movement.	• *Sergeant Early's Dream*: contrasting dynamics in various sections

Earthbound	Dancing with the body weight moving into or near the ground. There may be jumps but the emphasis is on the landing rather than on the time spent in the air.	• Section 9: *Sergeant Early's Dream* • Section 3: *Sergeant Early's Dream*
Elevation	Light, jumpy movement which may also involve large leaps.	• Section 4 *Lonely Town, Lonely Street* • Act 2 *Swan Lake* – various by swans on lake
Expressive Dance	Dance that uses the whole body and movement to express an idea, mood, story or emotion.	• *Sergeant Early's Dream*: throughout • *Swan Lake*: throughout
Flex	Turning the toes and foot up towards the ceiling.	• Section 9: *Sergeant Early's Dream*
Floor Patterns	The patterns and lines that dancers trace on the floor, through the travelling of their movements.	• Found in all masterworks listed. A good start would be Act 2 *Swan Lake* – swans on lake
Flow	How movements and phrases link together to form a whole dance.	• Section 2 *Sergeant Early's Dream* • Section 3 *Lonely Town, Lonely Street*
Fluid	Flowing movements that join together seamlessly.	• Act 2 *Swan Lake* – swans on lake
Focus	Looking with confidence and purpose. Imperative for performance.	• Section 1 *Lonely Town, Lonely Street* • Act 2 *Swan Lake* – lead swan solo
Free	A movement that has no definite finishing point, leading straight into the next movement e.g. a flung arm or swing. Contrasts with 'Bound'.	• *Sergeant Early's Dream*: various

Genre	A specific style of dance with a codified technique or set of ideals e.g. Ballet, Contemporary, Jazz.	• Act 1 *Swan Lake* – nightclub scene : rock n' roll influence • *Sergeant Early's Dream*: Irish folk influence • various in *Three by Rambert*
Gesture	A movement with no transfer of weight. Frequently preoccupied with the arms and hands.	• Act 1 *Swan Lake* – opening scene
Graham	American dancer/ choreographer. A pioneer of contemporary dance. In dance terms her influence is equal to Stravinsky and Picasso's in music and art. Own technique now used widely in dancers' training (source: *Dance Handbook*, 1990, p. 67).	• *Lonely Town, Lonely Street*: throughout – influence of Graham technique
Highlight	A moment of particular interest and excitement within a dance.	• Most works will demonstrate highlights
Jazz Dance	A genre that originated in Black America, involving isolations, little use of devices and a degree of sensuality. Widely used in commercial work and musicals.	• Influence seen throughout *Lonely Town, Lonely Street*
Levels	High, medium and low. Effective when used in contrast in duets and group dances.	• Section 1 *Sergeant Early's Dream* • Act 2 *Swan Lake* – swans on lake
Linear	Clear and strong lines, usually used to describe positions of the arms, legs and to describe floor patterns.	• Section 1 *Lonely Town, Lonely Street* • Act 2 *Swan Lake* – swans on lake
Lyrical	Light, fluid movement. Often slightly elevated.	• Section 2 *Sergeant Early's Dream* • Section 5 *Sergeant Early's Dream*

Motif	A short phrase or movement that represents the essence of the dance. Usually repeated and/or developed later on.	• Act 2 *Swan Lake*: – swans on lake: wings, head rolls, dipping, beak motifs
Motif Development	The development or a motif, how it changes e.g. slow it down, change the level etc.	• Act 2 *Swan Lake* – swans on lake •*Swan Lake*: throughout
Narrative	Movement that tells a story.	• *Lonely Town, Lonely Street*: various sections
New Dance	'A mini revolution which started (in the 1970s)…partly about choreographic experiment and partly about altering the way people think about dance…open to a wide range of influences and ideas' (Mackrell, J 1992, p1).	• *Strange Fish* (Newson, 1992) • *Flesh & Blood* (Anderson, 1991)
Organic	Where one movement grows out of another.	•*Sergeant Early's Dream*: throughout • Section 3 *Lonely Town, Lonely Street*
Parallel	Feet an inch or so apart, toes facing the front.	• Sections 1 & 2 *Sergeant Early's Dream*
Percussive	Movement (usually footwork) that is rhythmic, bound, earthbound and centred. Frequently making noise with the feet.	•Act 1 *Swan Lake* – nightclub scene • Act 2 *Swan Lake* – comedy swan quartet
Performance	Showing a dance for an audience – the best you can do. Qualities needed include confidence, focus, energy, thinking ahead, visual communication, listening skills.	• Any masterwork will demonstrate the qualities required for performance eg. *Witness*
Phrase	A sequence of movements.	

Plié	A bend of the knees with the feet in place on the floor, forming a diamond shape in between. May be in parallel or turned out with the feet in one of the five positions. A balletic term.	• All ballets show the use of plié as a transitory position. • Section 3: *Sergeant Early's Dream*
Projection	Letting the energy flow out of the movement, using a strong focus. Projecting towards a partner and/or audience.	• Section 1 *Intimate Pages* • Act 2 *Swan Lake* – swan/prince duet
Quality	How you dance rather than what you do. Paying attention to detail, sustaining movement, focus and confidence, not cutting corners.	• Any masterwork will demonstrate quality
Quartet	A dance for four people.	• Act 2 *Swan Lake* – comedy swan quartet
Release	A technique within the contemporary dance genre involving relaxing into the movement, releasing body tension, working within the capabilities of the body and using breath control. Now influencing a large amount of work.	• *Strange Fish* (Newson, 1992) • *Wyoming* (Davies, 1989)
Repetition	Repeating movements and phrases either intact or developed.	•Section 4: *Lonely Town, Lonely Street* • Act 3 *Swan Lake* – final scene
Social Dance	Dancing for fun, usually involving communities e.g. discos, barn dances, country dances, etc. Also embraces Folk Dance. Both can be used as a basis for Theatre Dance.	Social/Folk Dance as stimulus for Theatre Dance: • *Sergeant Early's Dream* – folk • Act 2 *Swan Lake* – nightclub scene: rock n' roll

Solo	A dance for one person.	•Section 6 *Lonely Town, Lonely Street* •Section 2 *Sergeant Early's Dream* • Act s 2 & 3 *Swan Lake* – lead swan/ball guest
Spatial awareness	Being aware of your own space, where others are in space, anticipating collisions etc.	
Spotting	The process which stops you falling over when turning. Looking at a spot in front of you until your body is turned 90°, then whipping the head round to look at it again.	• Act 2 *Swan Lake* – lead swan solo
Staccato	Sharp, strong, punctuated, stabbing movement.	• Section 1: *Lonely Town, Lonely Street* • Act 2 *Swan Lake* – nightclub scene
Stage left	The area to the left of you as you face the audience.	
Stage right	The area to the right of you as you face the audience.	
Stimulus	The starting point for the dance idea. May be music, a picture, a story, a mood etc.	*Swan Lake* – story, music *Lonely Town, Lonely Street* – film, book *Sergeant Early's Dream* – music, lyrics
Sustained	Stretching a movement to its very limit before moving to the next.	• Section 3: *Sergeant Early's Dream*
Symmetry	Movements or patterns that are the same on both sides.	• Act 2 *Swan Lake* swans on lake
Technique	Skill. A codified way of doing set exercises in order to build strength, stamina and facility. Codified techniques include Ballet, Graham, Cunningham.	

Tension	Controlled contracted energy held within the body. Various degrees of tension may be used.	• Section 1: *Lonely Town, Lonely Street*
Ternary Form	A dance taking the form of verse, chorus, verse, chorus etc or ABA	
Theatre Dance	Dances that are made specifically for an audience. Usually, although not always, performed in a theatre.	• All masterworks are examples of Theatre Dance
Tilt	A two-dimensional bend to the side from above the waist. Movement must be centre. Usually accompanied by linear and/or curved arms. Cunningham-based	• Act 2 *Swan Lake* – swans on lake • *Sergeant Early's Dream* throughout
Transition	A linking movement or phrase. The link between phrases	
Trio	A dance for three people	
Triplets	3 walks: Down, up, up. Repeated on alternate sides and travelling forwards, backwards, sideways or using a combination. Centred. Graham & Cunningham-based.	• Section 9: *Sergeant Early's Dream* • Section 4: *Lonely Town, Lonely Street*
Turnout	Turning the legs out from the hip sockets with the thighs, knees and toes aligned	• *Intimate Pages*: various • *Swan Lake*: throughout
Unison	Dancing altogether at the same time, usually using the same movement for maximum effect	• Section 1 & 4 *Lonely Town, Lonely Street* • Act 2 *Swan Lake* – swans on lake
Upstage	The area towards the back of the stage	• Used effectively in ball scene Act 3 *Swan Lake*

Laban's Effort table

Laban's Eight Basic Efforts

Effort	Time	Weight	Space
Punch	sudden	firm	direct
Float	sustained	light	flexible
Flick	sudden	light	flexible
Dab	sudden	light	direct
Press	sustained	firm	direct
Glide	sustained	light	direct
Slash	sudden	firm	flexible
Wring	sustained	firm	flexible

Further reading

Dance Books Ltd have a very wide selection of dance books, videos, DVDs and music. It is an excellent starting point if you are beginning to build up some resources for dance.

Dance Books Ltd
The Old Bakery
4 Lenten Street
Alton
Hampshire GU34 1HG
www.dancebooks.co.uk
01420 86138

Further reading

Dance UK	*Dance Teaching Essentials* ISBN 0-9515631-3 (2002)	Dance UK
Mackrell, J	*Out of Line* (1992)	Dance Books
Robertson, A. & Hutera, D.	*The Dance Handbook* (1988)	Longman
Sherborne, V	*Developmental Movement For Children (2001)* ISBN 0-903-26904-0	Worth Publishing
Shreeves, R	*Children Dancing* (1990) ISBN 0-7062-4988-7	Ward Lock Educational
Smith-Autard, J	*The Art Of Dance In Education* (2002) ISBN 0-7136-6175-5	A & C Black Publishers, London

Video/DVDs

Three by Rambert – 3 pieces: *Lonely Town, Lonely Street, Intimate Pages* & *Sergeant Early's Dream* (see glossary). Arthaus Musik.
Swan Lake by Mathew Bourne (Adventures in Motion Pictures – see glossary). Warner Music Vision.
A Tribute to Alvin Ailey – 4 pieces: *For Bird With Love, Witness, Memoria, Episodes*. Arthaus Musick.
Teaching Dance in The Primary School (1998) National Dance Teachers' Association.
Essential Alston – extracts and discussion of 3 pieces by Richard Alston. Contemporary Dance Trust from Dance Books.
Short Pinch Music to accompany T*he Dance Teacher's Survival Guide*, by D.M. Woodgate

Resource finder

Dance Organisations

National Dance Teachers Association
www.ndta.org.uk

National Resource Centre For Dance
01483 689316
www.surrey.ac.uk/NRCD
E-mail: NRCD@surrey.ac.uk

Council for Dance Education and Training
020 7247 4030
www.cdet.org.uk

Dance UK
020 7228 4990
www.danceuk.org

Royal Academy of Dance
020 7223 0091
www.rad.org.uk

Laban Centre
020 8691 8600
www.laban.org

Dance Agencies

Association of National Dance Agencies
www.anda.org.uk

Dance East
www.danceeast.co.uk

dance North west
www.dancenorthwest.co.uk

South East Dance
www.southeastdance.co.uk

Yorkshire Dance
www.yorkshiredance.org.uk

Swindon dance
www.swindondance.com

Dance Base (Scottish National centre For Dance)
www.dancebase.co.uk

Dance 4
www.dance4.co.uk

Dance City
www.dancecity.co.uk

The Place (London)
www.theplace.org.uk

east london dance
www.eastlondondance.org

Companies

There is an extensive list of dance companies with a description of their work and education services offered at www.londondance.com

Transitions Dance Company, Laban
020 8691 8600
www.laban.org

Phoenix Dance Theatre
0113 242 3486
www.phoenixdancetheatre.co.uk

Rambert Dance Company
0208 630 0600
www.rambert.org.uk

Union Dance
0207 724 5765
www.uniondance.co.uk

Adzido Pan African Dance Ensemble
020 7359 7453
www.adzido.com

Akram Khan
020 7401 7337
faroog.c@virgin.net

Useful websites

www.dfes.gov.uk	Government Music and Dance Scheme
www.artsmark.org.uk	national educational award
www.dancenetwork.org.uk	Best Practice Dance Network